BARIATRIC AIR COOKBOOK

Mouthwater Recipes To Bariatric Diet With Deliciously Satisfying Bariatric-Friendly Air Fryer Dishes with 30 Days Easy & Flavorful Meal Plan

SILVY COOPER

Table of Contents

BONUSES 7

INTRODUCTION 8

GENERAL OVERVIEW OF BARIATRIC SURGERY 8

THE VARIOUS TYPES OF BARIATRIC SURGERY PROCEDURES 8

The Roux-En-Y Gastric Bypass 9

Laparoscopic Sleeve Gastrectomy 9

The Adjustable Gastric Band 10

THE IMPORTANCE OF PROPER DIET AFTER SURGERY 10

BASIC CONCEPTS OF THE BARIATRIC DIET 12

Phase 1: Clear Liquids 12

Phase 2: Full Liquids 12

Phase 3: Pureed Soft Foods 12

Phase 4: Regular Consistency 12

WHAT FOODS SHOULD BE AVOIDED AFTER SURGERY 13

OVERVIEW OF THE AIR FRYER 13

What is the Air Fryer? 13

How Does it Work? 13

Benefits Using the Air Fryer 14

Cooking Tips & Tricks 14

Air Fryer Cleaning & Maintenance 15

CHAPTER 1: BREAKFAST 16

1.SHRIMP FRITTATA 16

2.POTATOES WITH BACON 16

3.INDIAN CAULIFLOWER 17

4.BREAKFAST FRITTATA 17

5.PEPPER EGG BITES 18

6.CAULIFLOWER MIX BLACK COD 18

7.KALE WITH TUNA 19

8.ONION OMELET 19

9.SPINACH EGG BREAKFAST 20

10.BROCCOLI MUFFINS 20

11.SHRIMP SANDWICHES 21

12.GARLIC BACON PIZZA 21

13.POTATO JALAPENO HASH 21

14.BREAKFAST CASSEROLE 22

15.ASPARAGUS SALAD 23

16.VEGETABLE QUICHE 23

17.BREAKFAST FISH TACOS 24

18.CHICKEN & ZUCCHINI OMELET 24

19.ZUCCHINI GRATIN 25

20.SPICY SWEET POTATO HASH 25

CHAPTER 2: LUNCH 26

21.SNAPPER & SPRING ONIONS 26

22.GROUND CHICKEN MEATBALLS 26

23. CHEESY SCOTCH EGGS 27

24.CRUMBLY CHICKEN TENDERLOINS 27

25.GARLIC HERB TURKEY BREAST 28

26.AIR FRIED CHICKEN FILLETS 28

27.SPICY SHRIMP 29

28.FLOUNDER FILLETS 29

29.STEAK WITH CABBAGE 30

30.PARSLEY CATFISH 30

31.CORNISH CHICKEN 31

32.JAPANESE-STYLE FRIED PRAWNS 31

33.STUNNING AIR-FRIED CLAMS 32

34.PACKET LOBSTER TAIL 32

35.RANCH FISH FILLETS 33

36.SWEET & SOUR CHICKEN 33

37.SESAME SEEDS COATED FISH 34

38.MIND-BLOWING AIR-FRIED CRAWFISH WITH CAJUN DIPPING SAUCE 34

39.HEALTHY CHICKEN CASSEROLE 35

40.VINEGAR SPICE PRAWNS 36

CHAPTER 3: DINNER **37**

41.HERBED TROUT & ASPARAGUS 37

42.MONTREAL FRIED SHRIMP 37

43.CHICKEN DRUMSTICKS 38

44.HERB FLAVORED LAMB 38

45.SPICED TILAPIA 39

46.LIME AIR FRYER SALMON 39

47.GRILLED TILAPIA WITH PORTOBELLO MUSHROOMS 40

48.HERBED BAKED SHRIMP 40

49.LEMON & CHICKEN PEPPER 41

50.CAJUN CHICKEN 41

51.LEMON-PEPPER CHICKEN BREAST 42

52.CHICKEN DRUMETTES 43

53.AIR FRYER CHILI LIME TILAPIA 43

54.LEMON CHICKEN BREAST 44

55.GRILLED SARDINES 44

56.EASY TUNA PATTIES 45

57.TARRAGON CHICKEN 45

58.CHICKEN WITH CITRUS SAUCE 46

59.HEALTHY SAUSAGE MIX 46

60.CAJUN SALMON 47

CHAPTER 4: VEGETABLES **48**

61.CRISPY BROCCOLI 48

62.CHARD WITH CHEDDAR 48

63.CORN ON COBS 49

64.CRISPY BRUSSELS SPROUTS AND POTATOES 49

65.SALTY LEMON ARTICHOKES 50

66.CHEESY ROASTED SWEET POTATOES 50

67.SOY SAUCE MUSHROOMS 51

68.CREAMY CABBAGE 51

69.DILL MASHED POTATO 52

70.MUSHROOMS WITH VEGGIES & AVOCADO 52

71.AIR FRIED LEEKS 53

72.CREAMY POTATOES 53

73.ASPARAGUS WITH GARLIC 54

74.CHILI SQUASH WEDGES 54

75.CREAM POTATO 55

CHAPTER 5: SNACKS **56**

76.BAKED POTATOES 56

77.CHEESY CHICKEN ROLLS 56

78.BANANA SNACK 56

79.TASTY CHEESE STICKS 57

80.CHEESE STICKS 58

81.COCOA BANANA CHIPS 58

82.SWEET APPLE & PEAR CHIPS 59

83.DELICIOUS MUSHROOM MIX SIDE DISH 59

84.BLENDED VEGGIE CHIPS 60

85.AVOCADO JALAPENO SIDE DISH 60

86.HEALTHY SPINACH BALLS 61

87.DELICIOUS WRAPPED SHRIMP 62

88.CHEESY CHICKEN WINGS 62

89.APPETIZING CAJUN SHRIMP 63

90.PARTY PORK ROLLS 63

CHAPTER 6: MEAT **64**

91.AIR-FRIED TURKEY BREAST 64

92.CHICKEN TIKKA MASALA 64

93.BASIL CHICKEN 64

94.GARLIC CHICKEN WINGS 65

95.LOW-CARB FRIED CHICKEN 65

96.CHICKEN FAJITAS 66

97.CREAMY CHICKEN 67

98.HONEY-LIME CHICKEN WINGS 67

99.CHICKEN HASH 67

100.PECAN CRUSTED CHICKEN 68

101.CHICKEN THIGHS 69

102.KOREAN FRIED CHICKEN 69

103.CHICKEN PAPRIKA 70

104.TURKEY MEATBALLS 70

105.CHICKEN KEBABS 71

CHAPTER 7: FISH **72**

106.MONKFISH WITH OLIVES & CAPERS 72

107.SPLENDID SALMON PATTIES 72

108.LEMON TUNA 73

109.SHRIMP, ZUCCHINI & CHERRY TOMATO SAUCE 73

110.SPINACH WITH SALMON & SEASHELLS 74

111.BUTTERED SCALLOPS 74

112.BASIL COD 74

113.CAJUN SPICED SALMON 75

114.SIMPLE SALMON 75

115.SEASONED CATFISH 76

116.GARLIC LEMON SHRIMP 76

117.SHRIMP & GREEN BEANS 77
118.SOUTHERN-AIR-FRIED CATFISH 77
119.COD FISH NUGGETS 78
120.CABBAGE WITH SALMON FISH 78

CHAPTER 8: DESSERTS **79**
121.RICOTTA CHEESECAKE 79
122.ANGEL FOOD CAKE 79
123.APPLE TREAT WITH RAISINS 80
124.AIR FRIED BANANA WITH SESAME SEEDS 80
125.CHOCOLATE SOUFFLÉ 80
126.BAKED APPLES 81
127.CHOCOLATE & POMEGRANATE BARS 82
128.APPLE HAND PIES 82
129.BERRY YOGURT CAKE 82
130.COCOA & ALMOND BARS 83
131.APPLE DUMPLINGS 83
132.CHOCOLATE MUG CAKE 84
133.GLAZED BANANAS 84
134.BLUEBERRY PUDDING 85
135.AIR FRIED APPLES 85
136.CHOCOLATE CAKE 86
137.CHERRY-CHOCO BARS 86
138.BERRIES MIX 87
139.CARROT CAKE 87
140.BLUEBERRY LEMON MUFFINS 88

CHAPTER 9: LIQUIDS **89**
141.HEALTHY BEAN SOUP 89
142.ONION SOUP 89
143.ASIAN PORK SOUP 90
144.BASIL TOMATO SOUP 90
145.ROASTED TOMATO SOUP 91
146.AIR FRYER BEAN SOUP 91
147.CHICKEN RICE NOODLE SOUP 92
148.COCONUT LIME SOUP 92
149.KALE BEEF SOUP 93
150.CORN SOUP 94

CONVERSION CHART **95**

30-DAY MEAL PLAN **97**

CONCLUSION **98**

INDEX **99**

BONUSES

Download Your 3 Exclusive Bonuses Now!

You've just unlocked a world of bariatric delights. To make your journey even more exceptional, we've prepared 3 amazing bonuses just for you. Here's how to easily claim them:

1. **Scan the QR Code below with your smartphone's camera.**
2. **Instantly access your exclusive bonuses.**

Take advantage of these extra tools to enrich your post-bariatric culinary adventure!"

Introduction

General Overview of Bariatric Surgery

If you've been dealing & struggling with obesity for years & have exhausted every solution in the book, bariatric surgery is one choice to consider.

Bariatric surgery is typically recommended when dieting & exercise haven't helped improve a person's health to an adequate degree. The procedure, which may involve a gastric bypass or sleeve gastrectomy, helps reduce the size of your stomach so that food can only be consumed in small amounts at a time. As after-surgery meals are limited to 600 calories per day, it becomes much easier to lose weight than when consuming 2,000 calories per day.

Bariatric surgery is recommended for people with a body mass index (BMI) of 40 or higher, or those with a BMI of 36 or higher who also have hypertension, diabetes, or heart disease.

The most common form of bariatric surgery is gastric bypass. It reduces the amount of food that your stomach can hold by creating a small pouch at the top of your stomach. The pouch connects directly to your small intestine to decrease the time it takes for food to move through your digestive system. This procedure typically results in short-term weight loss, followed by the potential for long-term weight control. As part of post-surgery care, you must learn to eat differently & should seek nutritional counseling for further guidance.

While weight loss is the main target of many on a bariatric diet, it can also help prevent several health problems including diabetes & heart disease. A bariatric diet is based on eating smaller meals more frequently, cutting out most processed food, & eliminating sugar. However, there are still ample amounts of fruits, vegetables, eggs, & protein in a bariatric diet which will provide you with the important nutrients you need.

The proper type of diet for someone embarking on bariatric surgery is often advised by the clinic or surgeon based on the patient's medical history, diagnosis, & overall health. Before making any final decisions or changes in diet or activity patterns, consult with your doctor first to establish a bariatric lifestyle that works best for you.

A little-known fact is that there are pre-surgery lifestyle changes that you can make to dramatically reduce your chances of developing the most common complications. This can include diet changes, supplements, & physical exercise.

The Various Types of Bariatric Surgery Procedures

The RYGB, the LSG, & the AGB are the three procedures that make up the majority of bariatric surgeries performed nowadays. Each bariatric surgeries are effective in reducing hunger & making it easier to limit section sizes. Nevertheless, certain surgeries operate at a further deeper metabolic level. It has been demonstrated that certain operations may enhance comorbid conditions such as type 2 diabetes, high blood pressure, sleep apnea, & fatty liver disease. The knowledge & experience of both your surgeon & the rest of your medical team is going to be required in order to arrive at the treatment option that is most suitable for you. Although every procedure comes with its own set of benefits & drawbacks, in the end, you will feel more in charge of your health thanks to all of them. Relax knowing that opting for any of the available surgical procedures was absolutely the right choice for you at this point in time.

The Roux-En-Y Gastric Bypass

This technique, more often referred to as gastric bypass, is regarded as the "gold standard" when it comes to surgical methods of weight loss. The process consists of two distinct phases: Your surgical team is going to start by creating a small stomach pouch with a volume of approximately one oz., & then they might divide the small intestine. After that, a direct connection is made between the pouch & the bottom portion of the small intestine. When food gets swallowed, it goes straight from the stomach pouch to the lower section of the small intestine, skipping over the majority of the stomach as well as the first section of the small intestine.

Advantages

- Reduces the amount of food that can be eaten & the capacity of the stomach
- Modifies gastrointestinal hormones in a beneficial way, resulting in decreased hunger & increased satiety
- Influences the amount of energy expended, which could help with maintaining & losing weight
- Should the need arise, reversible
- Possibility of large long-term excess weight loss (between sixty & eighty percent) with maintenance of over fifty percent of the lost weight

Disadvantages

- Rates of surgical complications that are significantly higher in comparison to those associated with gastric sleeve & band surgeries
- There is a significant possibility of developing vitamin & mineral deficiencies over time
- The lengthiest stays in the hospital
- There is a high potential for the development of food intolerances as well as dumping syndrome

Laparoscopic Sleeve Gastrectomy

Patients who undergo the Sleeve procedure are going to have approximately eighty percent of their stomachs resected while they are under the supervision of their respective surgical teams. The surgery is successful because it reduces the quantity of food that the stomach is able to store at any given moment; after the procedure, there is only a small, tubular pouch that is shaped like a banana. However, the most significant impact that it has is on the hormones in the gut that are responsible for hunger, satiety, & the regulation of blood sugar.

Advantages

- Reduces the amount of food that can be eaten & the ability of the stomach
- Modifies gastrointestinal hormones in a beneficial way, resulting in decreased hunger & increased satiety
- In comparison to gastric bypass, this procedure has a lower incidence of surgical complications
- In comparison to gastric bypass, there is a lower risk of dumping syndrome
- Does not need the insertion of an external device (like a gastric band) or the rerouting of the digestive tract (like a gastric bypass)
- Gastric bypass surgery is associated with fewer stays in the hospital
- Chance of a substantial reduction in extra weight (one that is larger than fifty percent)

Disadvantages

- Possible deficiency in vitamin & mineral intake over the long run
- Opportunities for acid reflux
- Nonreversible

The Adjustable Gastric Band

The surgery known as gastric banding involves placing an inflatable band around the top of the stomach in order to generate a tiny pouch in the stomach. Feeding the band with saline through a port hidden in the abdominal wall allows for a steady reduction in the size of the pouch that may be achieved through the course of time. The ease with which food can flow from the tiny pouch into the lower stomach is affected by the degree to which the band is tightened in this manner. The pouch is made to reduce feelings of hunger while simultaneously enhancing a sense of fullness.

Advantages

- Decreases the capacity of the stomach & restricts food intake
- Without making any incisions in the intestines or the wall of the stomach, this procedure is fully customizable & reversible
- the fewest early post-operative complications following surgical procedures
- the lowest possible risk for shortages in vitamins & minerals
- quickest lengths of hospital stays
- Causes average weight loss of between forty & fifty percent of extra weight

Disadvantages

- Early weight loss that is both slower & less significant compared to gastric bypass & band operations
- entails the maintenance of an implanted foreign device inside the body
- There is a possibility of problems, such as band slippage & erosion
- Patients who consume too much run the risk of having their esophagus become dilated
- There is a possibility of acquiring intolerances to particular dietary textures
- It is necessary to have a greater number of follow-ups in order to modify the band
- The greatest number of further surgical procedures

The Importance of Proper Diet After Surgery

The goal of bariatric nutrition is to tailor a high-calorie diet to the patient, in an effort to promote weight loss. It is generally prescribed for patients with a Body Mass Index (BMI) of 40 or higher. A normal BMI ranges from 18.5 - 24.9, & a person who has a BMI over 30 is generally considered obese.

With proper bariatric nutrition, you can lose about one pound every week without changing anything else about your lifestyle or diet choices that may sometimes help you lose weight at a slower rate or not at the entire. However, weight loss doesn't come from diet alone. A low-calorie diet works because it sets up your metabolism to burn off extra calories, which are stored as fat. Metabolism is an overall function of the body that converts food into energy.

A healthy lifestyle with proper nutrition is important for everyone, but especially for those who are seeking bariatric surgery, as bariatric surgery itself can make you put on weight again. These patients need to be aware of what they must do to maintain a healthy lifestyle after bariatric surgery so they can prevent putting on the additional weight & regain their quality of life.

While bariatric surgery can help reduce weight, patients should not discontinue eating a healthy diet for the long term. The changes in eating after surgery can cause serious complications, including putting on additional pounds & experiencing a loss of appetite that slows down weight loss. It also may cause problems with the intestines & digestive system. Patients who have been through bariatric surgery should follow a healthy diet plan under the supervision of their healthcare provider to maintain their weight loss & prevent putting on pounds or becoming malnourished. In addition, patients should be advised about how to maintain a healthy lifestyle after bariatric surgery so they can continue to eat a nutritious diet even when they're not going to the hospital every day for an office visit.

Bariatric Nutrition Before & After Surgery

Before Surgery: Before surgery, patients need to learn how to eat properly. This includes learning what types of calorie-rich foods they should eat, as well as the number of calories they should eat each day. They will also need to learn how to weigh themselves at home & calculate their Body Mass Index (BMI). If they are overweight, then it is likely that their BMI will be above 30. Patients who are obese may have a BMI that is over 40.

After Surgery: It takes time after weight loss surgery to learn how to eat properly. Learning how to eat the right quantity of calories every day can take weeks or even months. This means that patients will need to understand that there is no special diet or fad diet recommended for their weight loss after bariatric surgery. They are expected to follow any diet plan they are told by their doctors, but must continue eating healthy foods that are low in fat & saturated fat, as well as high in fiber & fruits & vegetables.

Practical Tips for Bariatric Diet

Patients on a bariatric diet lose more weight than persons on other types of diets, according to a number of studies. However, the bariatric diet is not just about losing weight; it is also about maintaining a healthy lifestyle. You can follow these practical tips to make sure you stay healthy at the entire times.

1. **Eat a variety of foods**

A diet that is high in nutrients will help ensure that you have the entire the vitamins & minerals your body needs. To ensure that you obtain the entire of the vitamins & minerals your body requires, consume a variety of foods from various dietary categories. This is important because some nutrients will not be present in many of the foods that are stapled on a bariatric diet. Keeping up with dietary fiber, protein, calcium, iron & vitamin D, between other nutrients is going to be very important for bariatric patients.

2. **Include exercise in your lifestyle**

Exercising is important for weight loss as it helps burn calories & thus control weight gain. However, exercise is more than just weight loss. Apart from helping you control your weight; exercise can also help boost your metabolism & give you more energy. Breathing exercises are also important for weight loss. When you're on a diet, it's easy to hold your breath, but breathing exercises can aid digestion, metabolism, & stress relief.

3. **Avoid alcohol while you are on a diet**

While some studies have shown that alcohol has little effect on bariatric patients who are on a low-carb diet, it is still not advised for them to consume large amounts of alcohol during the first months after surgery. Alcohol slows down the digestive process & thus decreases your body's ability to digest food optimally. In addition, alcohol may increase your caloric intake. It is best to limit your alcohol consumption to a glass or two of wine.

4. Remember not to skip meals

The real challenge of a bariatric diet is maintaining good nutrition & avoiding hunger pangs at the same time. The brain needs fuel & bariatric patients often feel weak & lightheaded if they go too long without eating due to the low-calorie/high-fiber nature of their intake. That's why it is important not to skip meals as this will only further impact your energy levels as well as promote hunger pangs that could lead you into making unhealthy choices such as snacking on high calories foods or binge eating.

Basic Concepts of The Bariatric Diet

Below is the outline of the diet progression of most bariatric surgery patients. However, everyone is different & should progress at a different speed or according to the doctor's directions.

Phase 1: Clear Liquids

Once the surgery is complete, the first phase of the bariatric diet begins. It would help if you tried as hard as possible to stay hydrated using a clear liquid such as water, broth, or unsweetened gelatin. This may sound challenging but will get easier & comfortable with time. You may try these tricks:

- Sip liquids constantly
- Have diluted juices such as grapes, apple, or cranberry juice
- Avoid extremely cold or hot liquids

Phase 2: Full Liquids

Usually, you can advance to this stage after five days. This phase involves foods with smooth or yogurt consistency. Some of the full liquids you may take are sugar-free protein shakes, thin broths, strained creamed soups, pudding, or no-fat yogurt. Below are some tricks to us in this phase:

- Take protein supplements after each meal to meet your set protein requirements.
- Don't drink at least 30 mins before meals.
- Take protein supplements or shakes 30 mins after meals.

Phase 3: Pureed Soft Foods

If it's two weeks since you underwent the bariatric surgery, you can incorporate pureed foods into your diet. The food should have a smooth paste consistency & should not have chunks or be fatty.

To achieve the right food consistency, you may chew thoroughly or blend food items with milk, water, broth, or sugar-free juices. Some of the foods you should overcook are veggies, beans, eggs, lean meat, soft fruits, yogurt, low-fat cheese.

Remember to stay hydrated by sipping fluids frequently & having a water bottle everywhere.

Phase 4: Regular Consistency

This phase starts six weeks after the bariatric surgery. You should eat three well-balanced, nutritious meals per day, taking a lot of fluids in between. You should also avoid empty calories & continue with supplements.

Make sure to try one food at a time to test what food your body can & can't tolerate. You can also load on a protein shake after a high-protein meal to meet the daily protein requirement.

What Foods Should Be Avoided After Surgery

Foods with empty calories

These include sweets, pastries, rice cakes, popcorns, chips, & pretzels. Most of these foods are loaded with sugar & fat may cause dumping syndrome that causes nausea, vomiting, diarrhea, or cold sweats.

Dry foods

You may consider avoiding dry foods till later after the bariatric surgery. Some of these dry foods are nuts, seeds, or granola. Otherwise, you may take cereals softened by low-fat milk.

When the time is right to consume dry foods, try small amounts at a time. If your body doesn't tolerate them, do not be discouraged, you will be able to eat the foods later.

Alcohol

Alcohol will take up the space of your little stomach that should be filled with essential nutrients such as proteins, vitamins, & minerals. Moreover, the alcohol absorption tends to be drastic after the bariatric surgery, thus leading to intoxication.

Pasta, bread, & rice

Avoid pasta, bread, & rice due to their starchy nature, making them hard to swallow. These foods may also block the stoma posing a risk to your health. You don't have to avoid them wholly, but it's advisable to avoid them in the first phases of your bariatric diet.

Fibrous vegetables & fruits

As aforementioned, it is advisable to eat nutritious foods such as vegetables & fruits. However, it's wise to avoid fibrous vegetables such as corn, celery, cabbage, broccoli, & asparagus.

High-fat food

Fatty foods such as sausage, bacon, whole milk, & butter will make you nauseous or cause dumping syndrome. Instead, consume low-fat meat, poultry, & low-fat cheese.

High sugar & caffeinated drinks

These drinks while on the bariatric diet may lead to dumping syndrome. Caffeine may also cause dehydration. Otherwise, take water, decaffeinated coffee, or other unsweetened beverages.

Overview of the Air Fryer

What is the Air Fryer?

The air fryer is a multifunction kitchen appliance that can give the same crispy results of deep-frying just by using hot air & a tiny amount of oil. It is quite an affordable tool, considering it can also grill, bake, & roast.

How Does it Work?

The air fryer is just like a countertop convection oven, only better & faster. This kitchen gadget features a heating element & a fan that facilitate the rapid circulation of hot air, cooking the food to crispy perfection.

Instead of deep-frying foods, the air fryer uses hot air to induce the Maillard reaction or the phenomenon that gives food its browning color & distinct taste & smell.

Best of the entire, the air fryer comes with dishwasher-safe parts & accessories, so you get deep fried-like goodness without the usual greasiness & mess.

Benefits Using the Air Fryer

Benefit #1: It is a beginner's treat! You can locate your favorite recipes & whip up a memorable meal at home in half of the time. The machine does the hard work for you. All you need to do is to include the temp. & times.

Benefit #2: Safety Functions: The machine will automatically shut down when the cooking time is completed. You will have fewer burned or overheated food items. The fryer will not slip because of the non-slip feet, which help eliminate the machine's risk of falling off the countertop. The closed cooking system helps prevent burns from hot oil or other foods.

Benefit #3: No Oily Clean Up: You only need to remove the cooking container, drip pan, or cooking basket. It is inside a cover which means you won't have oil vapor deposits on the walls, floors, or countertops. You can use the dishwasher to clean the movable parts. You can also use a sponge to clean the bits of food that might be stuck to the AF surfaces.

Benefit #4: The Fryer Needs Less Oil: It won't be necessary to include oil to the cooker if you have frozen products meant for baking. You only need to adjust the timer & cook. All of the excess fat will drip away into a tray beneath the basket.

You can cook whatever meats you relish & receive delicious & healthy results. You will understand this once you begin trying out some of these new recipes. For example, you can cook French fries with a tbsp of oil versus a vat of oil. It is possible to splurge on the more expensive oils since you only use such a minimal amount.

Benefit #5: Multitasking Features: The Air Fryer is capable of functioning as so many products, whether you need an oven, a hot grill, a toaster, a griddle, or a deep fryer—it is your answer! It can be used for breakfast, lunch, dinner, desserts, & even snacks.

Cooking Tips & Tricks

Give your air fryer enough time to pre-heat. Just set the timer for 2 or 3 mins after turning the air fryer on & setting your desired temp..

You may be tempted to cook one large batch of food at a time, but don't. Overcrowding the basket of the air fryer often leads to unevenly cook foods. It will also prevent food from crisping & browning. The food may take a longer time to cook, too.

Master the correct way of breading, step by step. We can't stress this enough: breading plays a vital role in many air fryer recipes. The fan of the air fryer can sometimes blow off the breading on the food. You must coat foods in three steps: flour, egg, & then breadcrumbs. Take an especially sweet time with the breadcrumbs, pressing them firmly onto the food.

The fan of the air fryer can also blow light & tiny food particles around, so it is best to secure foods with toothpicks.

Instead of drizzling or brushing oil on the food, use a spray bottle instead. It is not only easier but spraying oil also lets you keep the oil on the food to a minimum. Oil sprays in cans may have aerosol agents in them that can damage the non-stick surface of the air fryer basket so it will be worth it to invest in a hand-pumped kitchen spray bottle.

For an extra browning & crisping of food, spray it with oil halfway through the cooking time. The same timing for flipping foods will also yield more evenly cooked results.

To issue the components & flavor of the food, you may jiggle the basket from time to time the entire throughout the cooking process. This will also create more evenly browned & crisped dishes.

Include water to the air fryer drawer underneath the basket to avoid unnecessary smoking from the oil getting too hot while cooking.

You can open the air fryer as needed to check how the food is coming along. Rest assured that doing so will in no way interrupt the overall cooking process.

Now it is time to explore the many ways you can relish your meals. You have the basics of how to manage your diet after surgery. The recipes will guide you safely by providing you with the number of servings provided, how long it takes, & how much nutritional value is placed for the recipe.

Air Fryer Cleaning & Maintenance

Air fryers are great appliances for cooking healthier meals with less oil, but they do require regular cleaning & maintenance to function properly & avoid any hygiene issues. Below are some tips on how to clean & maintain your air fryer:

1. Unplug the air fryer then let it cool down prior to cleaning it.
2. Remove the basket or tray & wash it in warm soapy water. You can also put it in the dishwasher if it's dishwasher safe.
3. Wipe the inside of the air fryer with a wet sponge or cloth, but be careful not to use abrasive cleaners or scouring pads, as they may harm the non-stick coating.
4. The heating element should be cleaned using a soft-bristled brush or a toothbrush to prevent food particles from accumulating in it. Be gentle & avoid damaging the element.
5. Using a damp cloth or sponge, wipe the outside of the air fryer. In case of tough stains or oil, opt for a non-abrasive cleaner.
6. Make sure to dry the entire the parts of the air fryer thoroughly before reassembling it.
7. For maintenance, you should check the air fryer's manual for instructions on how to clean the fan & filter, as they can accumulate dust & oil over time.
8. It's important to regularly empty the oil tray or drawer to avoid any buildup that can cause smoking or unpleasant odors.

You can maintain the cleanliness & proper functionality of your air fryer for a long time by adhering to these guidelines, which in turn will enable you to prepare tasty & wholesome meals.

CHAPTER 1: Breakfast

1.SHRIMP FRITTATA

PREPARATION TIME	COOKING TIME	SERVING
10 mins	15 mins	2

INGREDIENTS	DIRECTIONS
<ul><li>4 eggs</li><li>half teaspoon basil, dried</li><li>Cooking spray</li><li>Salt & black pepper to the taste</li><li>half cup rice, cooked</li><li>half cup shrimp, cooked, skinned, deveined, & chopped</li><li>half cup baby spinach, chopped</li><li>half cup Monterey jack cheese, grated</li></ul>	1. Put eggs with salt, pepper, & basil in a container, then beat. 2. Oil your air fryer's pan with cooking spray & include rice, shrimp, & spinach. 3. Include eggs, mix, sprinkle cheese, & cook in your air fryer at 350 deg. F for 10 mins. 4. Split between plates & present for breakfast. Relish!

PER SERVING			
Calories: 162kcal	Fat: 6g	Carbs: 8g	Protein: 4g

2.POTATOES WITH BACON

PREPARATION TIME	COOKING TIME	SERVING
10 mins	20 mins	2

INGREDIENTS	DIRECTIONS
<ul><li>4 potatoes, skinned & cut into moderate cubes</li><li>4 bacon slices, chopped</li><li>2 rosemary springs, chopped</li><li>one tbsp olive oil</li><li>Salt & black pepper to the taste</li><li>2 eggs, beated</li></ul>	1. Combine oil with potatoes, bacon, rosemary, salt, pepper, & eggs in your air fryer's pan & beat. 2. Cook potatoes at 400 deg. F for twenty mins, split everything between plates, & present for breakfast. Relish!

PER SERVING			
Calories: 211kcal	Fat: 3g	Carbs: 8g	Protein: 5g

3. INDIAN CAULIFLOWER

PREPARATION TIME	COOKING TIME	SERVING
10 mins	20 mins	2

INGREDIENTS	DIRECTIONS
• three cups cauliflower florets • two tbsps. water • two tbsps. fresh lemon juice • half tbsp. ginger paste • 1 tsp. chili powder • ¼ tsp. turmeric • half cup vegetable stock • Pepper & salt	1. Include the entire components into the air fryer baking dish & combine thoroughly. 2. Put dish in the air fryer & cook at 400 deg. F for 10 mins. 3. Stir well & cook at 360 deg. F for 10 mins more. 4. Stir well & present.

PER SERVING			
Calories: 48kcal	Fat: 0.4g	Carbs: 8g	Protein: 4g

4. BREAKFAST FRITTATA

PREPARATION TIME	COOKING TIME	SERVING
15 mins	20 mins	2

INGREDIENTS	DIRECTIONS
• ¼ pound breakfast sausage, cooked & crumbled • half cup shredded Cheddar-Monterey Jack cheese blend • 1 onion, chopped • 2 tbsp red bell pepper, chopped • 4 eggs, beaten • Cooking spray	1. First, heat the air fryer to 370 deg. F. 2. Spray a cake pan with cooking spray. 3. Combine cheese, bell pepper, sausage, onion, & eggs in a container. Mix well. 4. Pour the mixture into the cake pan. 5. Bake in air fryer about 20 mins.

PER SERVING			
Calories: 310kcal	Fat: 21g	Carbs: 2g	Protein: 32g

5. PEPPER EGG BITES

PREPARATION TIME	COOKING TIME	SERVING
15 mins	15 mins	7

INGREDIENTS	DIRECTIONS
<ul><li>1/8 tsp. salt</li><li>⅓ cup bell pepper, minced, any color</li><li>half cup Colby cheese, shredded</li><li>half tsp. marjoram, dried</li><li>3 tbsp. scallions, minced</li><li>3 tbsps. milk</li><li>5 large eggs, beaten</li><li>Ground black pepper</li></ul>	1. Combine the milk, eggs, salt, marjoram, & black pepper in a moderate container. Mix till combined. 2. Stir in the scallions, bell peppers, & cheese. Fill the 7 egg bite cups with the egg mixture. Warm up the air fryer to 325 deg. F. 3. Make a foil sling: Fold an 18-inch-long piece of heavy-duty aluminum foil lengthwise into thirds. Put the egg bite pan on this sling & lower it into the air fryer. 4. Leave the foil in the air fryer, but bend down the edges so they fit in the appliance. 5. Bake the egg bites for 15 mins. 6. Use the foil sling to remove the egg bite pan. Let cool for 5 mins then invert the pan onto a plate to remove the egg bites. Present warm.

PER SERVING			
Calories: 87kcal	Fat: 6g	Carbs: 1g	Protein: 7g

6. CAULIFLOWER MIX BLACK COD

PREPARATION TIME	COOKING TIME	SERVING
6 mins	10 mins	1

INGREDIENTS	DIRECTIONS
<ul><li>1 cauliflower (chopped)</li><li>half tbsp. vinegar</li><li>Salt as required</li><li>1 lb. black cod (chopped)</li><li>For Sauce</li><li>half cup milk</li><li>half cup cheese</li><li>half cup basil</li></ul>	1. Include vinegar & salt to the air fryer pot. 2. Mix cauliflower & black cod chopped. 3. Cook at 300 deg. F for 15 mins. 4. Meanwhile, prepare sauce: mix milk, cheese, & basil. 5. Once ready, present by pouring the sauce over it to relish!

PER SERVING			
Calories: 100kcal	**Fat:** 10g	**Carbs:** 8g	**Protein:** 13.1g

7. KALE WITH TUNA

PREPARATION TIME	COOKING TIME	SERVING
4 mins	10 mins	1

INGREDIENTS	DIRECTIONS
<ul><li>12 cups Kale (chopped)</li><li>2 tbsp. lemon juice</li><li>1 tbsp. oil</li><li>1 can of tuna fish</li><li>1 tbsp. garlic (minced)</li><li>1 tsp. soy sauce</li><li>Salt & pepper as required</li></ul>	1. Include oil into the air fryer pot. 2. Mix tuna fish, garlic, soy sauce, lemon juice, kale, salt, & pepper. 3. Cook at 300 deg. F for 10 mins. 4. When ready, relish!

PER SERVING			
Calories: 90kcal	**Fat:** 8g	**Carbs:** 20g	**Protein:** 25g

8. ONION OMELET

PREPARATION TIME	COOKING TIME	SERVING
10 mins	15 mins	2

INGREDIENTS	DIRECTIONS
<ul><li>4 eggs</li><li>¼ tsp. low-sodium soy sauce</li><li>Ground black pepper, as required</li><li>1 tsp. butter</li><li>1 moderate yellow onion, sliced</li><li>¼ cup Cheddar cheese, grated</li></ul>	1. Start the recipe by melting the butter in a frying pan. 2. Next pour in & cook the onion for about ten mins. When it is cooked, set it aside to cool. 3. In a moderate-sized container, beat together the eggs, pepper & soy sauce. Include the cooled onion & mix everything together. 4. Pour this mixture into a small baking dish & put it in the air fryer. 5. Cook at 355 deg. F for about 5 mins. 6. When cooked, slice & present.

PER SERVING			
Calories: 221kcal	**Fat:** 14g	**Carbs:** 5.8g	**Protein:** 17g

9. SPINACH EGG BREAKFAST

PREPARATION TIME	COOKING TIME	SERVING
10 mins	20 mins	4

INGREDIENTS	DIRECTIONS
• 4 oz. fresh spinach, chopped • 3 eggs • ¼ cup milk, skimmed • 3 oz. cottage cheese • ¼ cup parmesan cheese, grated	1. Warm up your Air Fryer to 360 deg. F. 2. In a large container, include milk, eggs, half parmesan cheese, & cottage cheese. Beat well. Include the fresh spinach & stir well. 3. Carefully pour mixture into the air fryer baking dish. 4. Also sprinkle the remaining parmesan cheese on top. 5. Set dish in the air fryer. Cook for 20 mins. 6. Present!

PER SERVING			
Calories: 143kcal	**Fat:** 8.4g	**Carbs:** 2.4g	**Protein:** 15g

10. BROCCOLI MUFFINS

PREPARATION TIME	COOKING TIME	SERVING
10 mins	24 mins	4

INGREDIENTS	DIRECTIONS
• half tsp sea salt • 1 cup almond milk, unsweetened • 1 tsp. baking powder • 2 large eggs • 2 tbsps. nutritional yeast • cup broccoli florets, chopped • cups almond flour	1. First heat the air fryer to 325 deg. F for a few mins. 2. In a big container, include the entire components & mix till well combined. 3. Carefully & precisely pour the mixture into muffin molds & put them in the basket of the air fryer. 4. Bake the muffins for 20-24 mins. 5. Allow them to cool & then relish.

PER SERVING			
Calories: 260kcal	**Fat:** 21.2g	**Carbs:** 1g	**Protein:** 12g

11. SHRIMP SANDWICHES

PREPARATION TIME	COOKING TIME	SERVING
10 mins	5 mins	2

INGREDIENTS	DIRECTIONS
• one & ¼ cups cheddar, shredded • 6 oz. tiny shrimp, canned & drained • 3 tbsps. mayonnaise • 2 tbsps. green onions, chopped • 4 whole-wheat bread slices	1. In a container, mix the shrimps well with the cheese, green onion & mayonnaise. 2. Spread the mixture on half of the bread slices, cover with the other bread slices, & finally cut in half diagonally. 3. Put sandwiches in air fryer & cook at 350 deg. F for five mins. 4. Present.

PER SERVING

Calories: 161kcal	Fat: 2.6g	Carbs: 11g	Protein: 5g

12. GARLIC BACON PIZZA

PREPARATION TIME	COOKING TIME	SERVING
10 mins	13 mins	4

INGREDIENTS	DIRECTIONS
• Cooking spray • 4 dinner rolls • 1 cup of tomato sauce • 4 garlic cloves, minced • half tsp of garlic powder • 6 bacon slices, chopped • half tsp of oregano, dried • 1 1/4 cups of cheddar cheese, shredded	1. Spray dinner rolls & put them in the air fryer. 2. Cook for around 2 mins at 370 deg. F. 3. Include the entire the components on top & cook for around 8 mins at 370 deg. F. 4. Present & relish.

PER SERVING

Calories: 217kcal	Fat: 5g	Carbs: 12g	Protein: 4g

13. POTATO JALAPENO HASH

PREPARATION TIME	COOKING TIME	SERVING
25 mins	25 mins	4

INGREDIENTS	DIRECTIONS
• half tsp. ground cumin • 1 red bell pepper - sowed & chopped • half tsp. olive oil • half tsp. taco seasoning mix • 1 half lbs. potatoes - skinned & sliced • one jalapeno - sowed & sliced • one small onion - sliced • one tbsp. olive oil • Salt & black pepper	1. Put the potatoes in cold water. After twenty mins, drain them. 2. Season the potatoes using olive oil & disperse them in the Air Fryer. 3. Choose the Air Fry mode at 370 deg. F temp.. Cook for about 18 mins. 4. Meanwhile, in a big container, mix together olive oil, onion, peppers, taco seasoning & the entire other components. 5. Put this vegetable mixture in the basket & return to cooking. 6. Cook at 360 deg. F for about seven mins.

PER SERVING			
Calories: 241kcal	Fat: 14.4g	Carbs: 34g	Protein: 9.1g

14. BREAKFAST CASSEROLE

PREPARATION TIME	COOKING TIME	SERVING
10 mins	28 mins	4

INGREDIENTS	DIRECTIONS
• 2 eggs • 4 egg whites • 4 tsps. pine nuts, minced • ⅔ cup chicken broth • 1 lb. beef • ¼ cup red pepper, roasted & sliced • ¼ cup pesto sauce • 1/8 tsp. pepper • ¼ tsp. sea salt	1. Warm up the air fryer to 370 deg. F. Set aside the air fryer pan after spraying it with cooking spray. 2. Heat another pan over moderate heat. Include beef in a pan & cook till golden brown. 3. Once cooked, drain excess oil, & disperse it into the prepared pan. 4. Beat remaining components, except pine nuts, in a container & pour over sauce. 5. Cook for 25-28 mins in the air fryer with the pan. 6. Top with pine nuts & present.

PER SERVING			
Calories: 525kcal	Fat: 31g	Carbs: 2g	Protein: 39g

15. ASPARAGUS SALAD

PREPARATION TIME	COOKING TIME	SERVING
5 mins	10 mins	4

INGREDIENTS	DIRECTIONS
• 1 cup baby arugula • 1 bunch asparagus, trimmed • 1 tbsp. balsamic vinegar • 1 tbsp. cheddar cheese, grated • A tweak of salt & black pepper • Cooking spray, as needed	1. Put the asparagus in your air fryer's basket, oil with cooking spray, season with salt & pepper, & cook at 360 deg. F for 10 mins. 2. Take a container & mix the asparagus with the arugula & the vinegar. Toss, split between plates, & present hot with cheese drizzled on top.

PER SERVING			
Calories: 200kcal	Fat: 5g	Carbs: 4g	Protein: 5g

16. VEGETABLE QUICHE

PREPARATION TIME	COOKING TIME	SERVING
10 mins	25 mins	6

INGREDIENTS	DIRECTIONS
• 8 eggs • 1 cup tomatoes, chopped • 1 cup milk, skimmed • 1 onion, chopped • 1 cup zucchini, chopped • 1 tbsp. margarine • half tsp. pepper • 1 tsp. salt	1. First, heat the fryer to 370 deg. F. 2. In a griddle over moderate heat, sauté the onion with the oil till the onion is slightly brown. 3. Include the chopped tomatoes & zucchini. Sauté for 5 mins. 4. Transfer the vegetables to the air fryer pan. 5. In your container, beat the eggs with the cheese, milk, pepper & salt. 6. Pour this mixture over the vegetables. 7. Put the pan in the air fryer then bake for 25 mins. 8. Cut into slices & present.

PER SERVING			
Calories: 254kcal	Fat: 15g	Carbs: 7g	Protein: 23g

17. BREAKFAST FISH TACOS

PREPARATION TIME	COOKING TIME	SERVING
10 mins	13 mins	2

INGREDIENTS	DIRECTIONS
<ul><li>4 big tortillas</li><li>1 red bell pepper, chopped</li><li>1 yellow onion, chopped</li><li>4 white fish fillets, skinless & boneless</li><li>half cup salsa</li><li>A handful of mixed romaine lettuce, spinach, & radicchio</li><li>4 tbsp parmesan, grated</li></ul>	1. Put fish fillets in your air fryer & cook at 350 deg. F for 6 mins. 2. Meanwhile, heat a pan across moderate-high flame, include bell pepper & onion, stir & cook for 1-2 mins. 3. Organize tortillas on a working surface, split fish fillets, disperse salsa over them, split mixed veggies & greens, & disperse parmesan on each at the end. 4. Roll your tacos, put them in the warm upped air fryer then cook at 350 deg. F for six mins. 5. Split fish tacos between plates & present for breakfast. Relish!

PER SERVING			
Calories: 200kcal	Fat: 3g	Carbs: 9g	Protein: 5g

18. CHICKEN & ZUCCHINI OMELET

PREPARATION TIME	COOKING TIME	SERVING
15 mins	35 mins	2

INGREDIENTS	DIRECTIONS
<ul><li>8 eggs</li><li>¾ cup zucchini, chopped</li><li>1 cup chicken, cooked & chopped</li><li>half cup milk</li><li>1 cup Cheddar cheese, shredded</li><li>half cup chives, chopped</li><li>Salt & black pepper</li></ul>	1. Inside a container, beat well the milk, eggs, salt, & pepper. Mix & combine remaining components together as well. 2. Put the mixture in a oiled baking dish then select the "Air Bake" mode of the Air Fry oven. 3. Set the baking time to 35 mins & the temp. to 315 deg. F. 4. When warm upped, put the pan on the oven rack. 5. When cooked, slice & present.

PER SERVING			
Calories: 206kcal	Fat: 12g	Carbs: 2.1g	Protein: 10g

19. ZUCCHINI GRATIN

PREPARATION TIME	COOKING TIME	SERVING
10 mins	24 mins	4

INGREDIENTS

- 1 large egg, lightly beaten
- 1 ¼ cup almond milk, unsweetened
- 3 moderate zucchinis, sliced
- 1 tbsp. Dijon mustard
- half cup nutritional yeast
- 1 tsp. sea salt

DIRECTIONS

1. Warm up the air fryer to 370 deg. F.
2. Organize zucchini slices in the air fryer baking dish.
3. In a saucepan, heat almond milk over low heat & stir in Dijon mustard, nutritional yeast, & sea salt. Include beaten egg & beat well.
4. Top each zucchini with the mixture & cook for 20-24 mins.
5. Present & relish.

PER SERVING

Calories: 120kcal	Fat: 3.4g	Carbs: 14g	Protein: 13g

20. SPICY SWEET POTATO HASH

PREPARATION TIME	COOKING TIME	SERVING
10 mins	15 mins	4

INGREDIENTS

- 1 tbsp. paprika - smoked
- 1 tsp. dill weed - dried
- 1 tsp. black pepper
- 2 slices ham - cooked & chopped
- 2 sweet potato - chopped
- 2 tbsp. olive oil
- 1 tsp. sea salt

DIRECTIONS

1. Toss sweet potato with olive oil & the entire the spices in the Air Fry basket.
2. Cook for about 15 mins at 400 deg. F.
3. Flip the potatoes after every 5 mins.
4. Once done, toss in ham & present warm.

PER SERVING

Calories: 133kcal	Fat: 5.9g	Carbs: 36.3g	Protein: 6.8g

CHAPTER 2: Lunch

21. SNAPPER & SPRING ONIONS

PREPARATION TIME	COOKING TIME	SERVING
5 mins	14 mins	4

INGREDIENTS	DIRECTIONS
• 4 snapper fillets, boneless & skin scored • 6 spring onions, chopped. • Juice of half lemon • 3 tbsps. olive oil • 2 tbsps. sweet paprika • A tweak salt & black pepper	1. Take a container & mix the paprika with the rest of the components except the fish, & beat well. 2. Rub the fish with this mix, put the fillets in your air fryer's basket & cook at 390 deg. F for 7 mins on each side. Split between plates & present with a side salad.

PER SERVING			
Calories: 240kcal	Fat: 9g	Carbs: 6g	Protein: 13g

22. GROUND CHICKEN MEATBALLS

PREPARATION TIME	COOKING TIME	SERVING
10 mins	10 mins	4

INGREDIENTS	DIRECTIONS
• 1-lb. ground chicken • ⅓ cup panko • 1 tsp. salt • 2 tsps. chives • half tsp. garlic powder • 1 tsp. thyme • 1 egg	1. Toss the entire the meatball components in a container & combine thoroughly. Make small meatballs out of this mixture & put them in the air fryer basket. 2. Press the "Power Button" of the Air Fry Oven & turn the dial to select the "Air Fry" mode. Set the cooking time to 10 mins then the temp. at 350 deg. F. Once warm upped, put the air fryer basket inside & close its lid. Present warm.

PER SERVING			
Calories: 453kcal	Fat: 2.4g	Carbs: 18g	Protein: 23g

23. CHEESY SCOTCH EGGS

PREPARATION TIME	COOKING TIME	SERVING
5 mins	12 mins	2

INGREDIENTS

- 6 eggs
- 3/4 lb. of sausage
- 1/4 cup of parmesan cheese, shredded

DIRECTIONS

1. Warm up the air fryer to 390 deg. F. Boil eggs.
2. Peel eggs & set them aside.
3. Split sausage into equal portions.
4. Roll sausages with a wrap; it should look like a small pancake.
5. Wrap the egg in it. Do the same with the entire eggs.
6. Coat the outer surface with cheese.
7. Put these in an air fryer basket & cook for about 12 mins. Present & relish.

PER SERVING

Calories: 233kcal	Fat: 25g	Carbs: 23g	Protein: 20g

24. CRUMBLY CHICKEN TENDERLOINS

PREPARATION TIME	COOKING TIME	SERVING
7 mins	12 mins	4-8

INGREDIENTS

- 1 egg
- half cup dry breadcrumbs
- 2 tbsp. vegetable oil
- 8 chicken tenderloins

DIRECTIONS

1. Heat the air fryer to 350 deg. F.
2. Beat the egg in a small-sized mixing container.
3. Combine the breadcrumbs with the oil in a second container till the mixture is crumbly.
4. Dip the chicken into the container of the egg, shaking off any residual egg.
5. Dredge the chicken through the crumb mixture, making sure it's thoroughly covered.
6. Organize the tenderloins into the air fryer basket. Cook till the centers are no longer pink, about 12 mins.

7. The chickens' center should read at least 165 deg. F/74 deg. C when tested with a cooking thermometer.

PER SERVING			
Calories: 252kcal	Fat: 4g	Carbs: 9.8g	Protein: 26.2g

25. GARLIC HERB TURKEY BREAST

PREPARATION TIME	COOKING TIME	SERVING
10 mins	40 mins	6

INGREDIENTS	DIRECTIONS
• 1 tsp. rosemary • 1 tsp. thyme • 2 lbs. turkey breast • 3 cloves garlic • 4 tbsps. butter - melted	1. Mince the garlic & chop the rosemary & thyme. 2. Melt the butter & mix with the thyme, garlic, & rosemary in a mixing container. Brush this mixture over the turkey breast. 3. Put in the Air Fryer basket. Cook for 40 mins at 375 deg. F. Turn the turkey breast halfway through cooking. 4. Wait for 5 mins before slicing.

PER SERVING			
Calories: 281kcal	Fat: 19.3g	Carbs: 5g	Protein: 34g

26. AIR FRIED CHICKEN FILLETS

PREPARATION TIME	COOKING TIME	SERVING
10 mins	15 mins	3

INGREDIENTS	DIRECTIONS
• 2 eggs • 2 tbsp of vegetable oil • 12 ounces of chicken fillets • half teaspoon salt • 1 tsp of black pepper • 8 tbsp of breadcrumbs • 4 ounces of almond flour	1. Warm up the air fryer to 330 deg. F. 2. Mix oil, pepper, & salt in breadcrumbs & combine thoroughly. 3. Include chicken fillets into flour & then into the egg mixture. 4. Then coat with breadcrumb mixture. 5. Put these into sprayed air fryer basket. 6. Cook for about 15 mins at 390 deg. F. 7. Present & relish.

PER SERVING			
Calories: 162kcal	Fat: 4g	Carbs: 0g	Protein: 30g

27. SPICY SHRIMP

PREPARATION TIME	COOKING TIME	SERVING
5 mins	6 mins	8

INGREDIENTS	DIRECTIONS
<ul><li>2 tsps. old bay seasoning</li><li>1 tsp. cayenne pepper</li><li>1 tsp. paprika, smoked</li><li>4 tbsps. olive oil</li><li>2-lbs. tiger shrimp</li><li>Salt, as required</li></ul>	1. Include the entire the components in a large container. Mix well. 2. Warm up your Air Fryer to 390 deg. F then oil the air fryer basket. 3. Put shrimps in the basket & cook for about six mins. 4. Take out & present hot.

PER SERVING			
Calories: 173kcal	Fat: 7.9g	Carbs: 0.4g	Protein: 24g

28. FLOUNDER FILLETS

PREPARATION TIME	COOKING TIME	SERVING
10 mins	20 mins	4

INGREDIENTS	DIRECTIONS
<ul><li>4 flounder fillets, boneless</li><li>1 cup parmesan, grated</li><li>2 tbsps. olive oil</li><li>4 tbsps. butter, melted</li><li>Salt</li><li>Black pepper</li></ul>	1. Take a container & mix the parmesan with pepper, salt, butter, & oil, & stir well. 2. Organize the fish in a pan that fits the air fryer, disperse the parmesan mix the entire over, introduce in the fryer & cook at 400 deg. F for 20 mins. 3. Present & relish with a side salad.

PER SERVING			
Calories: 251kcal	Fat: 14g	Carbs: 6g	Protein: 12g

29. STEAK WITH CABBAGE

PREPARATION TIME	COOKING TIME	SERVING
10 mins	10 mins	4

INGREDIENTS	DIRECTIONS
<ul><li>2 tsp of cornstarch</li><li>1 tbsp of peanut oil</li><li>1 chopped yellow bell pepper</li><li>2 chopped green onions</li><li>2 minced garlic cloves</li><li>Salt & black pepper, as per taste</li><li>2 cups of chopped green cabbage</li><li>half pound of sirloin steak, chopped</li></ul>	1. Mix cabbage, peanut oil, black pepper, & salt in a container. 2. Put in the basket & cook for around 5 mins at 370 deg. F. 3. Include steak to the air fryer & mix the rest of the components. 4. Cook for around 5 mins. 5. Present with cabbage.

PER SERVING			
Calories: 282kcal	Fat: 6g	Carbs: 14g	Protein: 6g

30. PARSLEY CATFISH

PREPARATION TIME	COOKING TIME	SERVING
5 mins	25 mins	4

INGREDIENTS	DIRECTIONS
<ul><li>4 catfish fillets</li><li>¼ cup Louisiana Fish fry</li><li>1 tbsp. olive oil</li><li>1 tbsp. parsley, chopped</li><li>1 lemon, sliced</li><li>Fresh herbs, to garnish</li></ul>	1. Warm up the air fryer to 400 deg. F. 2. Rinse the fish fillets & pat, then fry. 3. Rub the fillets with the seasoning & coat well. Spray oil on top of each fillet. 4. Put the fillets in the air fryer basket & cook for ten mins. 5. Flip the fillets & cook more for another 10 mins. 6. Flip the fish & cook for 3 mins till crispy. 7. Garnish with parsley, fresh herbs, & lemon.

PER SERVING			
Calories: 248kcal	Fat: 15.7g	Carbs: 1.4g	Protein: 24.9g

31. CORNISH CHICKEN

PREPARATION TIME	COOKING TIME	SERVING
10 mins	25 mins	2

INGREDIENTS	DIRECTIONS
• Salt • Olive oil • 1 lemon • 1 Cornish chicken • Black pepper	1. Warm up the air fryer at390 deg. F. Coat, the chicken with olive oil. 2. Squeeze lemon inside it. Include any stuffing if you want. 3. Season it well with salt & pepper. Tie it with a string. 4. Spray the air fryer basket with olive oil. 5. Cook chicken for about 25 mins till golden brown. 6. Present & relish.

PER SERVING			
Calories: 566kcal	Fat: 45g	Carbs: 0g	Protein: 50g

32. JAPANESE-STYLE FRIED PRAWNS

PREPARATION TIME	COOKING TIME	SERVING
10 mins	15 mins	2

INGREDIENTS	DIRECTIONS
• 1 lb. prawns, skinned & deveined • 1 cup rice flour • 1 cup panko breadcrumbs • 2 eggs • 1 tsp. ground ginger • 1 tbsp. paprika • 1 tsp. salt • 1 tsp. black pepper • 1 tsp. garlic powder	1. Warm up your air fryer to 380 deg. F. 2. Using a container, include the prawns, salt, black pepper, garlic powder, ground ginger, & toss till it is properly mixed. 3. Then using another container, include the rice flour, paprika & mix it well. Pick a second container, include the eggs, & beat it properly. Then using a third container, include the panko breadcrumbs. 4. Dredge the seasoned prawns into the flour, dip it into the egg wash, & then cover it with the panko breadcrumbs. 5. Oil your air fryer basket with a nonstick cooking spray & include the prawns. 6. Cook it for 8 mins. 7. Present & relish!

PER SERVING

Calories: 210kcal	Fat: 8g	Carbs: 4g	Protein: 40g

33.STUNNING AIR-FRIED CLAMS

PREPARATION TIME	COOKING TIME	SERVING
10 mins	15 mins	2

INGREDIENTS	DIRECTIONS
• 1 (10-oz.) can whole baby clams, drained & shucked • 2 eggs, beaten • 1 cup flour • 1 cup panko breadcrumbs • 1 tsp. salt • 1 tsp. black pepper • 1 tsp. garlic powder • 1 tsp. onion powder • 1 tsp. cayenne pepper • 1 tbsp. oregano, dried	1. Warm up your air fryer to 390 deg. F. Using a container, include the flour; pick a second container, include the eggs, & mix properly. Then using a third container, include & mix the panko breadcrumbs, seasonings, & the herbs properly. 2. Dredge the clams in the flour, immerse it into the egg wash, & then cover it with the breadcrumb mixture. 3. Put the clams inside your air fryer & cook it for 2 mins or till it has a golden-brown color, while being cautious of overcooking. 4. Thereafter, carefully remove it from your air fryer & allow it to cool. Present & relish!

PER SERVING

Calories: 255kcal	Fat: 12g	Carbs: 3g	Protein: 15g

34.PACKET LOBSTER TAIL

PREPARATION TIME	COOKING TIME	SERVING
17 mins	12 mins	2

INGREDIENTS	DIRECTIONS
• 2 (6-oz.) lobster tails - halved • 2 tbsps. Butter - salted & melted • 1 tsp. parsley - dried • half tsp. Old Bay seasoning • Juice of half moderate lemon	1. On aluminum foil put the 2 halved tails. Season with Old Bay seasoning, butter & lemon juice. 2. Close the foil packets & put in the basket of the air fryer. 3. Set the temp. to 375 deg. F & the timer for 12 mins.

4. Sprinkle with parsley.
5. Present & relish!

PER SERVING			
Calories: 234kcal	Fat: 19g	Carbs: 7g	Protein: 23g

35. RANCH FISH FILLETS

PREPARATION TIME	COOKING TIME	SERVING
5 mins	13 mins	4

INGREDIENTS	DIRECTIONS
<ul><li>¾ cup Panko, crushed</li><li>1 packet dry ranch-style dressing mix</li><li>4 tilapia salmon or other fish fillets</li><li>2 half tbsps. vegetable oil</li><li>2 eggs beaten</li><li>Herbs & chilies to garnish</li></ul>	1. First warm up your air fryer to 180 deg. F for five mins. 2. Mix ranch dressing with panko in a container. 3. Beat the eggs in a second container. 4. Dip the fish fillets in the egg, & then coat them evenly with the panko mixture. 5. Put the fillets in the basket & cook for 13 mins. 6. Present hot with herbs & chilies.

PER SERVING			
Calories: 301kcal	Fat: 12.2g	Carbs: 15g	Protein: 19g

36. SWEET & SOUR CHICKEN

PREPARATION TIME	COOKING TIME	SERVING
10 mins	10 mins	4

INGREDIENTS	DIRECTIONS
<ul><li>1 lb. chicken breast, skinned & sliced into cubes</li><li>half cup cornstarch</li><li>Cooking spray, as needed</li></ul>For the Sauce:<ul><li>2 tbsp. chili garlic paste</li><li>4 tbsp. mayonnaise</li><li>2 tbsp. rice vinegar</li></ul>	1. Coat the chicken cubes with the cornstarch. 2. Spray with oil. 3. Air-fry at 400 deg. F for 5 mins per side. 4. Mix the sauce components. 5. Toss the chicken in the sauce, then present.

- 6 tbsp. sweet chili sauce

PER SERVING			
Calories: 421kcal	Fat: 13.6g	Carbs: 49.3g	Protein: 27.4g

37. SESAME SEEDS COATED FISH

PREPARATION TIME	COOKING TIME	SERVING
10 mins	14 mins	28

INGREDIENTS	DIRECTIONS
<ul><li>half cup sesame seeds, toasted</li><li>half tsp. rosemary, dried & crushed</li><li>6 eggs</li><li>8 tbsps. olive oil</li><li>14 fish fillets, frozen (white fish of your choice)</li><li>half cup breadcrumbs</li><li>8 tbsps. plain flour</li><li>Salt & ground black pepper</li></ul>	1. Take three dishes, put flour in one, crack eggs in the other & mix the remaining components except for fillets in the third one. 2. Now, coat the fillets in the flour & dip them in the beaten eggs. 3. Then, dredge generously with the sesame seeds mixture. 4. Meanwhile, warm up the air fryer to 390 deg. F & line the air fryer basket with foil. 5. Organize fillets in the basket & cook for about 14 mins, flipping once in a middle way. 6. Present & relish.

PER SERVING			
Calories: 179kcal	Fat: 8.3g	Carbs: 15.6g	Protein: 7.7g

38. MIND-BLOWING AIR-FRIED CRAWFISH WITH CAJUN DIPPING SAUCE

PREPARATION TIME	COOKING TIME	SERVING
10 mins	10 mins	4

INGREDIENTS	DIRECTIONS
<ul><li>1 lb. craw-fish tail meat, cooked</li><li>1 egg, beaten</li><li>4 green onions, chopped</li><li>1 tsp. butter, melted</li><li>1 tsp. salt</li><li>1 tsp. cayenne pepper</li><li>1 tsp. black pepper</li></ul>	1. Warm up your air fryer to 380 deg. F. 2. Using a container, include the eggs, green onion, butter, salt, cayenne pepper, black pepper, & salt. 3. Include the panko breadcrumbs, bread flour, & pour in the crawfish, stirring it till it is properly covered.

- ⅓ cup panko breadcrumbs
- ⅓ cup bread flour

Sauce Ingredients:

- ¾ cup mayonnaise
- half cup ketchup
- 1 tsp. horseradish

4. Oil your air fryer basket with a nonstick cooking spray.
5. Include the battered crawfish inside your air fryer & cook it for 5 mins or till it has a golden-brown color.
6. Thereafter, using a container, include the mayonnaise, ketchup, horseradish, & mix properly.
7. Present & relish!

PER SERVING

Calories: 205kcal	Fat: 16g	Carbs: 5.8g	Protein: 29g

39.HEALTHY CHICKEN CASSEROLE

PREPARATION TIME	COOKING TIME	SERVING
20 mins	17 mins	6

INGREDIENTS	DIRECTIONS
<ul><li>1 cup of salsa</li><li>Cooking spray</li><li>2 tsp of chili powder</li><li>2 tsp of ground cumin</li><li>1 tbsp of garlic powder</li><li>6 chopped kale leaves</li><li>1 cup of tomato sauce</li><li>half cup of chopped cilantro</li><li>1 cup of quinoa, cooked</li><li>2 chopped jalapeno peppers</li><li>half cup of chopped green onions</li><li>12 ounces of black beans, canned</li><li>3 cups of mozzarella cheese, grated</li><li>3 cups of boiled chicken breast, shredded</li></ul>	1. Spray the dish with cooking spray & the entire components in it. Mix well. Cook in the air fryer for about 17 mins at 350 deg. F. 2. Present & relish.

PER SERVING

Calories: 365kcal	Fat: 12g	Carbs: 22g	Protein: 26g

40. VINEGAR SPICE PRAWNS

PREPARATION TIME	COOKING TIME	SERVING
5 mins	8 mins	1-2

INGREDIENTS

- 1 tbsp. ketchup
- 12 prawns, shelled & deveined
- 1 tbsp. white wine vinegar
- half tsp. black pepper
- half tsp. sea salt
- 1 tsp. chili flakes
- 1 tsp. chili powder

DIRECTIONS

1. Put Air Fryer Lid on top. Press Air Fry, set the temp. to 375 deg. F, & set the timer to 5 mins to warm up.
2. Take Air Fryer Basket, oil it with some cooking spray. In the basket, include the entire components & combine well.
3. Put the basket in the inner pot of the Instant Pot, & close the Air Fryer Lid on top.
4. Press the "Air Fry" setting. Set the temp. to 390 deg. F & set the timer to 8 mins. Press "Start." Stir mixture halfway down.
5. Open Air Fryer Lid after cooking time is over. Present warm.

PER SERVING

Calories: 178kcal	Fat: 3.1g	Carbs: 99g	Protein: 21g

CHAPTER 3: Dinner

41. HERBED TROUT & ASPARAGUS

PREPARATION TIME	COOKING TIME	SERVING
5 mins	14 mins	4

INGREDIENTS	DIRECTIONS
• 4 trout fillets, boneless & skinless • 1 bunch asparagus, trimmed • ¼ cup chives & tarragon, mixed • 2 tbsps. ghee, melted • 2 tbsps. olive oil • 1 tbsp. lemon juice • Salt • Black pepper	1. In a container mix asparagus with half the oil, pepper & salt. Finally cook them in the basket of your air fryer at 380 deg. for 6 mins. 2. While cooking, in the same container, season the trout with salt, pepper, lemon juice, the rest of the oil, & the herbs. 3. Cook the fillets in the basket at 380 deg. F for 7 mins per side. 4. Taste the fish fillet with the asparagus.

PER SERVING			
Calories: 230kcal	Fat: 11g	Carbs: 4g	Protein: 9g

42. MONTREAL FRIED SHRIMP

PREPARATION TIME	COOKING TIME	SERVING
5 mins	8 mins	6

INGREDIENTS	DIRECTIONS
• 1-lb.raw shrimp, skinned & deveined • 1 egg white 3 tbsp. • half cup the entire-purpose flour • ¾ cup panko breadcrumbs • 1 tsp. paprika • 1 tbsp. Montreal Chicken Seasoning, as required • Salt & pepper • Cooking spray	1. Warm up the Air Fryer to 400 deg. F. Toss the shrimp with Montreal seasonings. 2. Beat egg whites in a container. Keep the breadcrumbs & flour in separate containers. 3. First, dredge each shrimp in the flour, then dip into the egg whites, & then coat with the breadcrumbs. Put the coated shrimps in the air dryer & spray the cooking oil over them. 4. Air fry for about 4 mins, then flip the shrimps. 5. Continue cooking for another 4 mins. Present warm.

PER SERVING			
Calories: 248kcal	**Fat:** 2.4g	**Carbs:** 12.1g	**Protein:** 44.3g

43. CHICKEN DRUMSTICKS

PREPARATION TIME	COOKING TIME	SERVING
10 mins	20 mins	8

INGREDIENTS	DIRECTIONS
• 8 chicken drumsticks • 2 tbsps. olive oil • 1 tsp. salt • 1 tsp. pepper • 1 tsp. garlic powder • 1 tsp. paprika • half tsp. cumin	1. Mix olive oil with salt, black pepper, garlic powder, paprika, & cumin in a container. 2. Rub this mixture over the entire the drumsticks. 3. Put these drumsticks in the Air fryer basket. Select the "Air Fry" mode. 4. Set the cooking time to 20 mins & the temp. at 375 deg. F. 5. Put the Air fryer basket inside the oven. 6. Flip the drumsticks when cooked halfway through. 7. Resume air frying for another rest of the 10 mins. Present warm.

PER SERVING			
Calories: 212kcal	**Fat:** 11.8g	**Carbs:** 4g	**Protein:** 19.3g

44. HERB FLAVORED LAMB

PREPARATION TIME	COOKING TIME	SERVING
10 mins	10 mins	4

INGREDIENTS	DIRECTIONS
• Salt • 1 rack of lamb • Pepper • 2 tbsp of dried rosemary • 1 tbsp of dried thyme • 4 tbsp of olive oil • 2 tsp of minced garlic	1. Mix herbs in a container along with oil. 2. Mix & coat lamb with it. 3. Put in the air fryer then cook for around 10 mins at 360 deg. F. 4. Present & relish.

PER SERVING			
Calories: 346kcal	Fat: 11g	Carbs: 23g	Protein: 34g

45. SPICED TILAPIA

PREPARATION TIME	COOKING TIME	SERVING
10 mins	12 mins	2

INGREDIENTS	DIRECTIONS
<ul><li>2 (6-ounce) tilapia fillets</li><li>¼ tsp garlic powder</li><li>¼ tsp onion powder</li><li>¼ tsp ground cumin</li><li>Cooking spray</li><li>Salt & black pepper</li><li>1 tbsp butter melted</li></ul>	1. Oil the basket of the air fryer with cooking spray then slide it inside. 2. Warm up the fryer to 370 deg. F for a few mins. 3. Stir in the salt, spices, & black pepper. 4. Season the fillets with oil & the spice mixture. 5. Put the tilapia fillets in the oiled basket of the air fryer. 6. Cook for twelve mins. 7. Turn the fillets halfway through cooking. 8. Present & relish.

PER SERVING			
Calories: 640kcal	Fat: 13g	Carbs: 1.9g	Protein: 101g

46. LIME AIR FRYER SALMON

PREPARATION TIME	COOKING TIME	SERVING
5 mins	8 mins	4

INGREDIENTS	DIRECTIONS
<ul><li>4 pieces salmon fillet,</li><li>1 tsp chili-lime seasoning</li><li>Salt</li><li>half tsp garlic powder</li><li>1 tbsp oregano</li><li>1 teaspoon smoked paprika</li><li>4 lime wedges</li><li>half cup chopped cilantro</li><li>Mango-avocado salsa</li></ul>	1. Season salmon with oil, garlic powder, chili-lime seasoning, paprika, salt & oregano. 2. Put salmon in oiled basket lined with baking paper. Bake at 400 deg. F for about 8 mins. 3. Present with lime wedges & some fresh cilantro.

PER SERVING			
Calories: 261kcal	**Fat:** 11g	**Carbs:** 1g	**Protein:** 39g

47. GRILLED TILAPIA WITH PORTOBELLO MUSHROOMS

PREPARATION TIME	COOKING TIME	SERVING
20 mins	5 mins	2

INGREDIENTS	DIRECTIONS
<ul><li>4 moderate-sized Portobello mushrooms</li><li>2 tilapia fillets</li><li>half tsp. red pepper flakes, crushed</li><li>half tsp. sage, dried & crushed</li><li>¼ tsp. lemon pepper</li><li>Salt</li><li>Parsley</li><li>1 tbsp. avocado oil</li><li>A few drizzles liquid smoke</li></ul>	1. Take a container & inside mix the entire the components except the mushrooms. 2. Season the tilapia fillets with the newly created mixture. 3. Warm up the air fryer to 400 deg. F then cook the tilapia fillets for 5 mins. 4. Include the Portobello mushrooms & turn the fillets over. Continue cooking for 5 mins. 5. Present & relish.

PER SERVING			
Calories: 320kcal	**Fat:** 11.4g	**Carbs:** 29.1g	**Protein:** 49.3g

48. HERBED BAKED SHRIMP

PREPARATION TIME	COOKING TIME	SERVING
5 mins	10 mins	4

INGREDIENTS	DIRECTIONS
<ul><li>1 tbsp. garlic, minced</li><li>2 tsps. red pepper flakes</li><li>4 tbsps. butter</li><li>1 tbsp. lemon juice</li><li>1 tbsp. chives, chopped</li><li>1 tbsp. basil leaves, minced</li><li>2 tbsps. chicken stock (or white wine)</li><li>1-lb. shrimp, defrosted</li></ul>	1. Put Air Fryer Lid on top. Press Air Fry, set the temp. to 375 deg. F, then set the timer to 5 mins to warm up. 2. Take Air Fryer Basket, oil it with some cooking spray. In the basket, include shrimp, butter. 3. Put the basket in the inner pot of the Instant Pot, & close the Air Fryer Lid on top.

4. Press the "Bake" setting. Set the temp. to 330 deg. F & set the timer to 2 mins. Press "Start."

5. Open Air Fryer Lid after cooking time is over. Mix in red pepper flakes & garlic.

6. Press the "Bake" setting. Set temp. to 330 deg. F & set the timer to 3 mins. Press "Start." Include other components & combine them.

7. Press the "Bake" setting. Set temp. to 330 deg. F & set the timer to 5 mins. Press "Start." Present warm.

PER SERVING			
Calories: 233kcal	Fat: 12g	Carbs: 3g	Protein: 23g

49. LEMON & CHICKEN PEPPER

PREPARATION TIME	COOKING TIME	SERVING
10 mins	5 mins	4

INGREDIENTS	DIRECTIONS
<ul><li>1 chicken breast</li><li>1 tbsp. chicken seasoning</li><li>1 tsp. garlic puree</li><li>2 lemons, juiced & rind</li><li>Handful peppercorns</li><li>Salt & pepper as required</li></ul>	1. Heat your air fryer to 352 deg. F. 2. Include the entire the seasonings along with the lemon zest to a large silver foil. 3. Remove fat & small bones from chicken breast. Season with pepper & salt. 4. Put the chicken on the silver foil & rub the seasoning well. Seal well. 5. Flatten with the help of a rolling pin. 6. Cook for 15 mins in your air fryer till the center is fully cooked. 7. Present!

PER SERVING			
Calories: 320kcal	Fat: 21g	Carbs: 5g	Protein: 32g

50. CAJUN CHICKEN

PREPARATION TIME	COOKING TIME	SERVING
10 mins	20 mins	8

INGREDIENTS	DIRECTIONS
• Cooking spray, as needed • 8 chicken drumsticks • Olive oil, as needed **For the Cajun Seasoning:** • 1 tsp. onion powder • 1 tsp. paprika • half tsp. garlic powder • half tsp. dried thyme • half tsp. dried basil • half tsp. dried oregano • half tsp. cayenne pepper • Salt & pepper, as required	1. Combine the Cajun seasoning components. 2. Spray the air fryer basket with oil. 3. Coat chicken with olive oil. 4. Sprinkle the entire sides of the chicken with the Cajun seasoning. 5. Include the chicken to the air fryer basket. 6. Cook at 400 deg. F for 10 mins per side.

PER SERVING			
Calories: 563kcal	Fat: 47.8g	Carbs: 1.8g	Protein: 25g

51. LEMON-PEPPER CHICKEN BREAST

PREPARATION TIME	COOKING TIME	SERVING
3 mins	20 mins	3

INGREDIENTS	DIRECTIONS
• 3 large chicken breasts • 1 large lemon, juiced & zested • 1 moderate lemon • 1 tsp. garlic powder • half tsp. sea salt • 2 tsp. ground black pepper	1. Heat the air fryer unit at 360 deg. F/182 deg. C. 2. Lay the chicken breasts out on a chopping board. 3. Smother them in the lemon juice & rind from your large lemon. Sprinkle it with the salt, garlic powder, & pepper. 4. Organize the breasts in the fryer basket. Cut the lemon slices & put them over the breasts (tops & sides). Air-fry for 15 mins. 5. Check the chicken & then cook further if they are still pink in the middle, about 3–5 mins. Slice the chicken breasts to present.

PER SERVING			
Calories: 276kcal	Fat: 6g	Carbs: 5g	Protein: 49g

52. CHICKEN DRUMETTES

PREPARATION TIME	COOKING TIME	SERVING
15 mins	15 mins	3

INGREDIENTS

- 3/4 tsp of brown sugar
- 1 tsp of sesame oil
- 3 tsp of prawn paste
- 1 tsp of ginger juice
- half tsp of Shaoxing wine
- half ounces of chicken drumettes
- 6 tsp of vegetable oil

DIRECTIONS

1. Mix the brown sugar, sesame oil, wine, ginger juice, & prawn paste to form the marinade.
2. Marinate chicken overnight in the fridge.
3. Warm up the air fryer for 5 mins at 356 deg. F.
4. Spray chicken with vegetable oil & put in an air fryer basket.
5. Cook for about 7 mins, turn the drumettes over & cook for another 8 mins till golden.
6. Present & relish.

PER SERVING

Calories: 90kcal	Fat: 7g	Carbs: 3g	Protein: 5g

53. AIR FRYER CHILI LIME TILAPIA

PREPARATION TIME	COOKING TIME	SERVING
5 mins	10 mins	2

INGREDIENTS

- 1 tsp cumin
- 1 tsp garlic powder
- half tsp salt
- 1/4 tsp black pepper
- 12 oz tilapia fillets
- 2 tsp chili powder
- Juice of 1 lime
- Lime zest

DIRECTIONS

1. Warm up the air fryer to 400 deg. F.
2. Oil the basket of the air fryer.
3. In a container, mix the entire the spices.
4. Season the fish with the spice mixture.
5. Put the fish in the air fryer & cook for ten mins.
6. Drizzle with lime juice & present.

PER SERVING

Calories: 171kcal	Fat: 2g	Carbs: 4g	Protein: 36g

54. LEMON CHICKEN BREAST

PREPARATION TIME	COOKING TIME	SERVING
10 mins	30 mins	4

INGREDIENTS	DIRECTIONS
<ul><li>¼ cup olive oil</li><li>⅓ cup dry white wine</li><li>1 & half tsps. Oregano - dried & crushed</li><li>1 lemon - sliced</li><li>1 tbsp. lemon zest - grated</li><li>1 tsp. thyme leaves - minced</li><li>2 tbsps. lemon juice</li><li>3 tbsps. garlic - minced</li><li>4 chicken breasts - skin-on boneless</li><li>Salt & pepper as required</li></ul>	1. Include the entire of the listed components to the pan. Put chicken breasts in as well & coat well. Include lemon slices on top. 2. Spread mustard mixture on the toasted bread slices. 3. Set the time to 30 mins & the temp to 370 deg. F. 4. Put the pan in the cooking basket of the air fryer & cook. 5. Present!

PER SERVING			
Calories: 302kcal	Fat: 7.1g	Carbs: 9g	Protein: 21g

55. GRILLED SARDINES

PREPARATION TIME	COOKING TIME	SERVING
5 mins	20 mins	4

INGREDIENTS	DIRECTIONS
<ul><li>5 sardines</li><li>Herbs of Provence</li><li></li></ul>	1. Warm up the air fryer to 320 deg. F. 2. Spray the basket & put your sardines in the basket of your fryer. 3. Set the timer for 14 mins. After 7 mins, remember to turn the sardines so that they are roasted on both sides.

PER SERVING			
Calories: 189kcal	Fat: 10g	Carbs: 10g	Protein: 22g

56. EASY TUNA PATTIES

PREPARATION TIME	COOKING TIME	SERVING
15 mins	10 mins	10

INGREDIENTS

- 1 stalk celery, chopped
- 1 tbsp lemon juice
- half cup bread crumbs
- half tsp dried oregano
- half tsp garlic powder
- 15 oz canned albacore tuna, drained
- 3 large eggs
- 3 tbsp grated parmesan cheese
- 3 tbsp minced onion
- Black pepper
- Salt

DIRECTIONS

1. In a container, combine the lemon zest, garlic powder, Parmesan cheese, lemon juice, eggs, bread crumbs, onion, celery, oregano, salt, & pepper.
2. Include the tuna & mix everything together well.
3. Create patties with this tuna mixture.
4. Line the basket of the air fryer with baking paper & organize the patties on top.
5. Bake at 360 deg. for about 10 mins.
6. Turn the patties halfway through cooking.
7. Present with lemon slices.

PER SERVING

Calories: 84kcal	Fat: 2.9g	Carbs: 2g	Protein: 15g

57. TARRAGON CHICKEN

PREPARATION TIME	COOKING TIME	SERVING
10 mins	15 mins	1

INGREDIENTS

- 1 chicken breast - skinless
- 0.125 tsp. ground black pepper
- 0.5 tsp. butter, unsalted
- 0.125 tsp. kosher salt
- 0.25 cup tarragon - dried

DIRECTIONS

1. Warm up the oven to reach 390 deg. F.
2. Organize the chicken in the foil with the tarragon, salt, butter & pepper.
3. Close the foil slightly to minimize airflow.
4. Air-fry the chicken packs for 12 mins in the basket.

PER SERVING

Calories: 84kcal	Fat: 5g	Carbs: 0.9g	Protein: 6g

58. CHICKEN WITH CITRUS SAUCE

PREPARATION TIME	COOKING TIME	SERVING
10 mins	12 mins	4

INGREDIENTS

- 2 tbsp of water
- 1 orange zest
- 2 tsp of cornstarch
- 1 tsp of soy sauce
- 2 tbsp of cornstarch
- half cup of orange juice
- 2 tbsp of brown sugar
- 1 tsp of rice wine vinegar
- 1 tsp of ground ginger
- Red pepper flakes
- 1 pound of boneless chicken breasts

DIRECTIONS

1. Warm up the air fryer to 400 deg. F.
2. Coat chicken with cornstarch.
3. Cook for 9 mins in the air fryer.
4. Mix & cook the entire the other components in a pan to make the sauce.
5. Include cornstarch & water to it & cook for about five more mins.
6. Present chicken with sauce & relish.

PER SERVING

Calories: 630kcal	Fat: 15g	Carbs: 46g	Protein: 75g

59. HEALTHY SAUSAGE MIX

PREPARATION TIME	COOKING TIME	SERVING
10 mins	10 mins	4

INGREDIENTS

- 2 tbsp of mustard
- 1 bell pepper. chopped
- 1/3 cup of ketchup
- half cup of chicken stock
- 3 tbsp of brown sugar
- half cup of chopped onion
- 1 pound of sliced sausages
- 2 tbsp of apple cider vinegar

DIRECTIONS

1. Mix the entire the components in a container.
2. Pour into the pan of the air fryer & cook for about 10 mins at 350 deg. F.
3. Present & relish.

PER SERVING

Calories: 162kcal	Fat: 6g	Carbs: 12g	Protein: 6g

60. CAJUN SALMON

PREPARATION TIME	COOKING TIME	SERVING
5 mins	10 mins	2

INGREDIENTS	DIRECTIONS
• 1 - 7 oz. salmon fillet 0.75-inches thick • Cajun seasoning • ¼ of a lemon juice • Optional: Sprinkle of sugar	1. Set the Air Fryer at 356 deg. Fahrenheit to warm up for five mins. 2. Rinse & dry the salmon with a paper towel. Cover the fish with the Cajun coating mix. 3. Put the fillet in the air fryer for seven mins with the skin side up. 4. Present with a sprinkle of lemon & a dusting of sugar if desired.

PER SERVING			
Calories: 285kcal	**Fat:** 17.8g	**Carbs:** 6.8g	**Protein:** 42.1g

CHAPTER 4: Vegetables

61. CRISPY BROCCOLI

PREPARATION TIME	COOKING TIME	SERVING
5 mins	15 mins	2

INGREDIENTS	DIRECTIONS
• 1 large head fresh broccoli • 2 tsps. olive oil • 1 tbsp. lemon juice	1. Rinse the broccoli & pat dry. Cut off the florets & separate them. You can also use the broccoli stems too; cut them into 1chunk & peel them. 2. Dress the broccoli with olive oil & lemon juice. 3. Cook the broccoli in the air fryer for about 12 mins or till broccoli is crispy. 4. Present!

PER SERVING			
Calories: 63kcal	Fat: 2g	Carbs: 10g	Protein: 4g

62. CHARD WITH CHEDDAR

PREPARATION TIME	COOKING TIME	SERVING
5 mins	15 mins	2

INGREDIENTS	DIRECTIONS
• 3 oz. cheddar cheese, grated • 10 oz. swiss chard • 3 tbsp. creams • 1 tbsp. sesame oil • Salt & pepper as required (very little	1. Wash Swiss chard carefully & chop it roughly. 2. Sprinkle the chopped chard with salt & ground pepper. 3. Stir it carefully. 4. Sprinkle Swiss chard with the sesame oil & stir it carefully with the help of 2 spatulas. 5. Warm up the air fryer to 260 deg. F. 6. Put chopped Swiss chard in the air fryer basket & cook for 6 mins. 7. Shake it after 3 mins of cooking. 8. Then pour the cream into the air fryer basket & mix it up. 9. Cook for 3 mins more. 10. Then increase the temp. to 400 deg. F.

11. Sprinkle with the grated cheese & bake for another 2 mins.
12. After this, transfer the meal to the serving plates. Relish!

PER SERVING

Calories: 172kcal	Fat: 22.3g	Carbs: 6.7g	Protein: 63.3g

63. CORN ON COBS

PREPARATION TIME	COOKING TIME	SERVING
10 mins	10 mins	2

INGREDIENTS	DIRECTIONS
• 2 fresh corns on cobs • 2 tsps. butter • 1 tsp. salt • 1 tsp. paprika • ¼ tsp. olive oil	1. First, warm up the air fryer to 400 deg. F. 2. Rub the corn on cobs with salt & paprika. Then sprinkle the corn on cobs with the olive oil, & put them in the air fryer basket. Cook for 10 mins. 3. When the time is over, transfer the corn on cobs to the serving plates & rub with the butter gently. 4. Present the meal immediately.

PER SERVING

Calories: 122kcal	Fat: 5.5g	Carbs: 17.6g	Protein: 3.2g

64. CRISPY BRUSSELS SPROUTS AND POTATOES

PREPARATION TIME	COOKING TIME	SERVING
10 mins	8 mins	2

INGREDIENTS	DIRECTIONS
• ¾ lb. brussels sprouts, washed & trimmed • half cup new potatoes, chopped • 2 tsp bread crumbs • Salt & black pepper • 2 tsps. butter	1. In a container, include Brussels sprouts, potatoes, bread crumbs, salt, pepper, & butter. Mix well. 2. Put in the air fryer basket then cook at 400 deg. F for 8 mins. 3. Present & relish!

PER SERVING

Calories: 152kcal	Fat: 3g	Carbs: 17g	Protein: 4g

65. SALTY LEMON ARTICHOKES

PREPARATION TIME	COOKING TIME	SERVING
15 mins	45 mins	1

INGREDIENTS	DIRECTIONS
<ul><li>1 lemon</li><li>2 artichokes</li><li>1 tsp. kosher salt</li><li>1 garlic head</li><li>2 tsp. olive oil</li></ul>	1. Cut off the edges of the artichokes. 2. Cut the lemon into halves. 3. Peel the garlic head & chop the garlic cloves roughly. 4. Then put the chopped garlic in the artichokes. 5. Sprinkle the artichokes with olive oil & kosher salt. 6. After that, squeeze the lemon juice into the artichokes. 7. Wrap the artichokes in the foil. 8. Warm up the air fryer to 330 deg. F. 9. Put the wrapped artichokes in the air fryer & cook for 45 mins. 10. When the artichokes are cooked, discard the foil & present. 11. Relish!

PER SERVING			
Calories: 133kcal	Fat: 5g	Carbs: 21.7g	Protein: 6g

66. CHEESY ROASTED SWEET POTATOES

PREPARATION TIME	COOKING TIME	SERVING
5 mins	20 mins	4

INGREDIENTS	DIRECTIONS
<ul><li>2 large sweet potatoes, skinned & sliced</li><li>1 tsp. olive oil</li><li>1 tbsp. white balsamic vinegar</li><li>1 tsp. thyme, dried</li><li>¼ cup Parmesan cheese, grated</li></ul>	1. In a big container, shower the sweet potato slices with the olive oil & toss. 2. Sprinkle with the balsamic vinegar & thyme & toss again. 3. Sprinkle the potatoes with the Parmesan cheese then toss to coat. 4. Roast the slices, in batches, in the air fryer basket for 20 mins, tossing the sweet potato slices in the basket once during cooking, till tender.

5. Repeat with the remaining sweet potato slices. Present immediately.

PER SERVING

Calories: 100kcal	Fat: 3g	Carbs: 15g	Protein: 4g

67. SOY SAUCE MUSHROOMS

PREPARATION TIME	COOKING TIME	SERVING
10 mins	12 mins	2

INGREDIENTS	DIRECTIONS
<ul><li>8 oz mushrooms, sliced</li><li>Cooking Spray</li><li>1 tsp soy sauce</li><li>2 tbsp avocado oil</li><li>Salt & black pepper</li></ul>	1. Oil the basket & warm up the air fryer to 380 deg. F for five mins. 2. In a container, include the entire components then combine thoroughly. 3. Put the mushrooms in the basket & cook for 10 mins. 4. Shake the basket while cooking. 5. Finally, present & relish.

PER SERVING

Calories: 120kcal	Fat: 13g	Carbs: 0.9g	Protein: 2g

68. CREAMY CABBAGE

PREPARATION TIME	COOKING TIME	SERVING
10 mins	20 mins	1

INGREDIENTS	DIRECTIONS
<ul><li>half green cabbage head, chopped</li><li>half yellow onion, chopped</li><li>Salt & black pepper, as required (very little)</li><li>half cup whipped cream</li><li>1 tbsp. cornstarch</li></ul>	1. Put cabbage & onion in the air fryer. 2. In a container, mix cornstarch with cream, salt, & pepper. Stir & pour over cabbage. 3. Mix well & then bake at 400 deg. F for 20 mins. 4. Present.

PER SERVING

Calories: 208kcal	Fat: 10g	Carbs: 16g	Protein: 55g

69.DILL MASHED POTATO

PREPARATION TIME	COOKING TIME	SERVING
10 mins	15 mins	2

INGREDIENTS

- 2 potatoes
- 2 tbsps. fresh dill, chopped
- 1 tsp. butter
- half tsp. salt
- ¼ cup half & half

DIRECTIONS

1. Warm up the air fryer to 390 deg. F.
2. Rinse the potatoes thoroughly & put them in the air fryer. Cook for 15 mins.
3. After this, remove them from the air fryer. Peel the potatoes.
4. Mash the potatoes with the help of the fork well. Then include chopped fresh dill & salt.
5. Stir it gently & include butter & half & half.
6. Take the hand blender & blend the mixture well.
7. Relish!

PER SERVING

Calories: 211kcal	Fat: 5.7g	Carbs: 36.5g	Protein: 5.1g

70.MUSHROOMS WITH VEGGIES & AVOCADO

PREPARATION TIME	COOKING TIME	SERVING
30 mins	8 mins	1

INGREDIENTS

- 10 ounces mushrooms, halved
- 1 garlic clove, minced
- 1 tbsp balsamic vinegar
- 1 yellow onion, chopped
- 1 tbsp olive oil
- Salt & black pepper
- 1 teaspoon basil, dried
- 1 avocado, skinned, pitted, & roughly cubed
- A tweak of red pepper flakes

DIRECTIONS

1. Mix the mushrooms with onion, garlic, & avocado in a container.
2. Mix the vinegar, oil, salt, pepper, & basil in another container & beat well.
3. Pour this over the vegetables, then toss to coat, set aside for 30 mins, transfer to the basket of your air fryer, & then cook at 350 deg. F for 8 mins,
4. Split between plates & present with pepper flakes on top as a garnish.

PER SERVING

Calories: 182kcal	Fat: 3g	Carbs: 5g	Protein: 8g

71. AIR FRIED LEEKS

PREPARATION TIME	COOKING TIME	SERVING
5 mins	7 mins	2

INGREDIENTS	DIRECTIONS
<ul><li>2 leeks, washed, ends cut, & halved</li><li>Salt & black pepper</li><li>half tbsp. butter, melted</li><li>half tbsp. lemon juice</li></ul>	1. Rub leeks with melted butter & season with pepper & salt. 2. Lay it inside the air fryer & cook at 350 deg. F for seven mins. 3. Organize on a platter. 4. Drizzle with lemon juice & present.

PER SERVING			
Calories: 99kcal	Fat: 4g	Carbs: 5.9g	Protein: 2g

72. CREAMY POTATOES

PREPARATION TIME	COOKING TIME	SERVING
12 mins	20 mins	2

INGREDIENTS	DIRECTIONS
<ul><li>¾ lb. potatoes, skinned & cubed</li><li>1 tbsp. olive oil</li><li>Salt & black pepper</li><li>half tbsp. hot paprika</li><li>half cup Greek yogurt</li></ul>	1. Put potatoes in a container, pour water to cover, & leave aside for ten mins. Drain, pat dry, & then transfer to another container. 2. Include salt, pepper, paprika, & half of the oil to the potatoes & mix. 3. Put potatoes in the air fryer basket & cook at 360 deg. F for 20 mins. 4. In a container, mix yogurt with salt, pepper, & the rest of the oil & beat. 5. Split potatoes onto plates, drizzle with yogurt dressing, mix, & present.

PER SERVING			
Calories: 170kcal	Fat: 3g	Carbs: 20g	Protein: 5g

73. ASPARAGUS WITH GARLIC

PREPARATION TIME	COOKING TIME	SERVING
5 mins	10 mins	4

INGREDIENTS	DIRECTIONS
• 1-lb. asparagus, rinsed, ends snapped off where they naturally break • 2 tsps. olive oil • 3 garlic cloves, minced • 2 tbsps. balsamic vinegar • half tsp. thyme, dried	1. In a big container, mix the asparagus with olive oil. Transfer to the air fryer basket. 2. Sprinkle with garlic. Roast for 8 to 11 mins for asparagus that is crisp on the outside & tender on the inside. 3. Drizzle with the balsamic vinegar & sprinkle with the thyme leaves. 4. Present & relish.

PER SERVING			
Calories: 41kcal	Fat: 1g	Carbs: 6g	Protein: 3g

74. CHILI SQUASH WEDGES

PREPARATION TIME	COOKING TIME	SERVING
10 mins	18 mins	2

INGREDIENTS	DIRECTIONS
• 11 oz. acorn squash • half tsp. salt • 1 tbsp. olive oil • half tsp. chili pepper • half tsp. paprika	1. Cut Acorn squash into the serving wedges. 2. Sprinkle the wedges with the salt, olive oil, chili pepper, & paprika. 3. Warm up the air fryer to 400 deg. F. Put Acorn squash wedges in the air fryer basket & cook for 18 mins. 4. Flip the wedges into another side after 9 mins of cooking. 5. Present the cooked meal hot. Relish!

PER SERVING			
Calories: 125kcal	Fat: 7.2g	Carbs: 16.7g	Protein: 1.4g

75. CREAM POTATO

PREPARATION TIME	COOKING TIME	SERVING
15 mins	20 mins	2

INGREDIENTS

- 3 moderate potatoes, scrubbed
- half tsp. kosher salt
- 1 tbsp. Italian seasoning
- ⅓ cup cream
- half tsp. ground black pepper

DIRECTIONS

1. Slice the potatoes. Warm up the air fryer to 365 deg. F.
2. Make the layer from the sliced potato in the air fryer basket.
3. Sprinkle the potato layer with the kosher salt & ground black pepper.
4. After this, make the second layer of the potato & sprinkle it with Italian seasoning.
5. Make the last layer of the sliced potato & pour the cream.
6. Cook the scallop potato for 20 mins.
7. When the scalloped potato is cooked, let it chill till the room temp. Relish!

PER SERVING

Calories: 269kcal	Fat: 3g	Carbs: 42.6g	Protein: 6.8g

CHAPTER 5: Snacks

76. BAKED POTATOES

PREPARATION TIME	COOKING TIME	SERVING
10 mins	1 hr	2

INGREDIENTS	DIRECTIONS
• half teaspoon coarse sea salt • 1 tbsp peanut oil • 2 large potatoes, scrubbed	1. Warm up your air fryer to 400 deg. F. Brush peanut oil on your potatoes & sprinkle some salt. Then keep them in the basket of your air fryer. 2. Cook the potatoes for an hr. Present hot.

PER SERVING

Calories: 360kcal	Fat: 8g	Carbs: 64g	Protein: 8g

77. CHEESY CHICKEN ROLLS

PREPARATION TIME	COOKING TIME	SERVING
20 mins	10 mins	12

INGREDIENTS	DIRECTIONS
• half cup tomato sauce • 12 egg roll wrappers • 2 celery stalks, finely chopped. • 2 cups chicken, cooked & chopped. • 2 green onions, chopped • 4 oz. blue cheese, crumbled • Cooking spray • Salt & black pepper - as required	1. In a container, mix chicken meat with blue cheese, green onions, salt, celery pepper, & tomato sauce. Stir well & keep in the fridge for 2 hrs. 2. Split the chicken mixture into the egg wrappers. Roll them up & seal the edges. 3. Put rolls in your air fryer's basket. Spray them with cooking oil & cook at 350 deg. F for 10 mins; flipping them halfway.

PER SERVING

Calories: 210kcal	Fat: 5.2g	Carbs: 13g	Protein: 11g

78. BANANA SNACK

PREPARATION TIME	COOKING TIME	SERVING
10 mins	5 mins	8

INGREDIENTS	DIRECTIONS
• 16 baking cups crust • ¼ cup peanut butter • ¾ cup chocolate chips • 1 banana, skinned & sliced into 16 pieces • 1 tbsp vegetable oil	1. Put chocolate chips in a small pot, heat up over low heat, stir till it melts & take off the heat. 2. In a container, mix peanut butter with coconut oil & beat well. 3. Spoon 1 teaspoon chocolate mix in a cup, include 1 banana slice, & top with 1 teaspoon butter mix. 4. Repeat with the rest of the cups, put them the entire into a dish that fits your air fryer, cook at 320 deg. F for 5 mins, transfer to a freezer & keep there till you present them as a snack. 5. Relish!

PER SERVING

Calories: 70kcal	Fat: 4g	Carbs: 10g	Protein: 1g

79. TASTY CHEESE STICKS

PREPARATION TIME	COOKING TIME	SERVING
1 hr and 10 mins	8 mins	4

INGREDIENTS	DIRECTIONS
• Cooking spray • 2 eggs, beated • 8 mozzarella cheese strings, cut into halves • 1 garlic clove, minced • 1 cup parmesan, grated • 1 tbsp. Italian seasoning • Salt & black pepper - as required	1. Mix parmesan cheese, pepper, salt, Italian seasoning, & garlic in a container. 2. Beat eggs in a second container. 3. Dip the mozzarella sticks first into the egg mixture & then into the first container's parmesan mixture. Repeat this step a second time & put them in the freezer for 1 hr. 4. Spray the cheese sticks with cooking oil. Cook them at 390 deg. F in the air fryer's basket for 8 mins. Turn them over after 4 mins.

PER SERVING

Calories: 140kcal	Fat: 5g	Carbs: 3g	Protein: 4g

80. CHEESE STICKS

PREPARATION TIME	COOKING TIME	SERVING
10 mins	10 mins	6

INGREDIENTS	DIRECTIONS
<ul><li>1 teaspoon garlic powder</li><li>1 teaspoon of Italian spices</li><li>¼ teaspoon rosemary, ground</li><li>2 eggs</li><li>1 cheese sticks</li><li>¼ cup parmesan cheese, grated</li><li>¼ cup whole-wheat flour</li></ul>	1. Unwraps the cheese sticks. Keep aside. Beat the eggs into a container. 2. Mix the cheese, flavorings, & flour in another container. 3. Now roll the sticks in the egg & then into the batter. Coat well. Keep them in your air fryer basket. 4. Cook for 7 mins at 370 deg. F. Present hot.

PER SERVING

Calories: 76kcal	Fat: 4g	Carbs: 5g	Protein: 5g

81. COCOA BANANA CHIPS

PREPARATION TIME	COOKING TIME	SERVING
5 mins	7 mins	4

INGREDIENTS	DIRECTIONS
<ul><li>¼ teaspoon cocoa powder</li><li>5 large firm bananas, skinned</li><li>A cinnamon powder tweaks</li></ul>	1. Warm up the air fryer in Dehydrate mode at 110 deg. F for 2 to 3 mins. On the other hand, utilize a mandolin slicer to very finely slice the bananas & coat them well with cocoa powder & cinnamon powder. In batches, organize as many banana pieces as possible in a single layer on the cooking tray. 2. When the device is ready, slide the cooking tray onto the top rack of the oven & close the oven set the timer to 7 mins, & press Start. Cook till the banana pieces are crispy. Transfer the chips to serving containers when the entire set & make the remaining in the same manner. Take pleasure in.

PER SERVING

Calories: 152kcal	Fat: 0.57g	Carbs: 38.89g	Protein: 1.87g

82. SWEET APPLE & PEAR CHIPS

PREPARATION TIME	COOKING TIME	SERVING
15 mins	10 mins	4

INGREDIENTS

- 6 pears, skinned
- 6 Honey crisp apples

DIRECTIONS

1. Warm up the air fryer in Dehydrate mode at 110 deg. F for 2 to 3 mins. On the other hand, utilize a mandolin slicer to very finely slice the apples & pears. In batches, set up a few of the fruit slices in a single layer on the cooking tray.
2. When the device is ready, move the cooking tray onto the top rack of the oven & close the oven
3. Set the timer to 7 mins then press Start. Cook till the fruits are crispy. Transfer the fruit chips to serving containers when the entire set & make them stay in the same manner. Take pleasure in.

PER SERVING

Calories: 142kcal	Fat: 0.46g	Carbs: 37.7g	Protein: 0.71g

83. DELICIOUS MUSHROOM MIX SIDE DISH

PREPARATION TIME	COOKING TIME	SERVING
4 mins	20 mins	1

INGREDIENTS

- ¼ cup oil
- ¼ cup flour (the entire-purpose)
- 1 bell pepper
- 1 onion (chopped)
- 2 cups chicken (chopped breast)
- 4.5 oz. mushrooms
- 4.5 oz. tomatoes – chopped
- 2 tsp. sauce (any)
- 3 garlic cloves

DIRECTIONS

1. Oil the baking tray with oil.
2. Include flour & chicken into a container.
3. Mix bell pepper, onion, mushrooms, tomatoes, sauce, garlic cloves, soy sauce, sugar, & hot sauce with salt & pepper.
4. Pour the mixture into the baking tray.
5. Cook in the air fryer for 20 mins at 300 deg. F.
6. When ready, present!

- 1 tsp. soy sauce
- 1 tsp. sugar (white)
- Salt & pepper as required
- 3 drops of hot sauce

PER SERVING			
Calories: 70kcal	Fat: 6g	Carbs: 10g	Protein: 10g

84. BLENDED VEGGIE CHIPS

PREPARATION TIME	COOKING TIME	SERVING
20 mins	10 mins	4

INGREDIENTS	DIRECTIONS
<ul><li>1 big carrot</li><li>1 teaspoon salt</li><li>1 teaspoon Italian spices</li><li>1 zucchini</li><li>1 sweet potato skinned</li><li>half teaspoon pepper</li><li>1 red beet, skinned</li><li>A tweak cumin powders</li></ul>	1. Warm up the air fryer in Dehydrate mode at 110 deg. F for 2 to 3 mins 2. Utilize a mandolin slicer to thinly slice the entire the vegetables & transfer them to a moderate container. Season it with salt, Italian spices, & cumin powder. In batches, organize some of the veggies in a single layer on the cooking tray. 3. When the device is ready, move the cooking tray onto the top rack of the oven & close the oven, then set the timer to 7 or 9 mins & press Start. Cook up till the veggies are crispy. Transfer the vegetables to serving containers when the entire set & make them stay in the same manner. Delight in.

PER SERVING			
Calories: 84kcal	Fat: 0.15g	Carbs: 18.88g	Protein: 2.25g

85. AVOCADO JALAPENO SIDE DISH

PREPARATION TIME	COOKING TIME	SERVING
3 mins	15 mins	1

INGREDIENTS	DIRECTIONS
• 4 avocados (skinned) • 2 tbsp. lime juice • 2 tbsp. lemon juice • 2 cans of tomatoes (chopped) • half cup red onion (chopped) • 1 large jalapeno pepper (minced) • 3 cloves garlic (minced) • Salt & pepper as required	1. Mash avocados into the container. 2. Mix lime juice, lemon juice, tomatoes, red onions, jalapeno pepper, & garlic with salt & pepper. 3. Pour the mixture into the air fryer & cook for 15 mins on high pressure. 4. When done, present & relish!

PER SERVING			
Calories: 91kcal	Fat: 4g	Carbs: 10g	Protein: 25.7g

86. HEALTHY SPINACH BALLS

PREPARATION TIME	COOKING TIME	SERVING
10 mins	7 mins	30

INGREDIENTS	DIRECTIONS
• 4 tbsp. butter, melted • 2 eggs • 1 cup flour • 1/4 tsp. nutmeg, ground • 1/3 cup parmesan, grated • 16 oz. spinach • 1/3 cup feta cheese, crumbled • 1 tbsp. onion powder • 3 tbsp. whipping cream • 1 tsp. garlic powder • Salt • Black pepper	1. In your blender, mix the entire the components. Blend very well & keep in the freezer for 10 mins. 2. Shape 30 spinach balls. Put them in your air fryer's basket & cook at 300 deg. F, for 7 mins. 3. Present as a snack.

PER SERVING			
Calories: 60kcal	Fat: 1.2g	Carbs: 1g	Protein: 2g

87. DELICIOUS WRAPPED SHRIMP

PREPARATION TIME	COOKING TIME	SERVING
15 mins	11 mins	16

INGREDIENTS	DIRECTIONS
• 10 oz. already cooked shrimp, skinned & deveined • 1/3 cup blackberries; ground • 11 prosciuttos sliced • 1 tbsp. mint; chopped. • 1/3 cup red wine • 2 tbsp. olive oil	1. Wrap each shrimp in a slices of ham & oil them with oil. 2. Put in warm upped air fryer at 390 deg. F for about 8 mins. 3. Heat a pan with the ground blackberries over low heat. Include the mint & wine. Cook for 4 mins. 4. Present & relish the shrimp with the sauce

PER SERVING			
Calories: 224kcal	Fat: 12.5g	Carbs: 7.5g	Protein: 18.8g

88. CHEESY CHICKEN WINGS

PREPARATION TIME	COOKING TIME	SERVING
10 mins	13 mins	6

INGREDIENTS	DIRECTIONS
• 6 lb. chicken wings, halved • 1 tsp. garlic powder • 1 egg • 2 tbsp. butter • A tweak of red pepper flakes, crushed • Salt & black pepper - as required • half tsp. Italian seasoning • half cup parmesan cheese, grated	1. Organize chicken wings in your air fryer's basket & cook at 390 deg. F for 10 mins. 2. In a blender, blend cheese, pepper, pepper flakes, butter, salt, egg, garlic powder, & Italian seasoning. 3. Take chicken wings out & pour cheese sauce over them & cook in your air fryer's basket at 390 deg. F for 3 mins.

PER SERVING			
Calories: 192kcal	Fat: 8.1g	Carbs: 14.5g	Protein: 16.2g

89. APPETIZING CAJUN SHRIMP

PREPARATION TIME	COOKING TIME	SERVING
10 mins	5 mins	2

INGREDIENTS

- 20 tiger shrimp, skinned & deveined
- half tsp. old bay seasoning
- 1 tbsp. olive oil
- 1/4 tsp. smoked paprika
- Salt
- Black pepper

DIRECTIONS

1. In a container, mix shrimp with oil, pepper, salt, old bay seasoning, & paprika & toss to coat.
2. Put shrimp in your air fryer's basket & cook at 390 deg. F for 5 mins.
3. Present & relish!

PER SERVING

Calories: 161kcal	Fat: 6g	Carbs: 8g	Protein: 16g

90. PARTY PORK ROLLS

PREPARATION TIME	COOKING TIME	SERVING
15 mins	35 mins	4

INGREDIENTS

- 1 (15 oz.) pork fillet
- half tsp. chili powder
- 1 tsp. cinnamon powder
- 1 red onion, chopped
- 3 tbsp. parsley, chopped
- 1 garlic clove, minced
- 2 tbsp. olive oil
- 1 half tsp. cumin, ground
- Salt & black pepper as required

DIRECTIONS

1. In a container, mix cinnamon with garlic, salt, pepper, chili powder, oil, onion, parsley, & cumin. Stir well
2. Put pork fillet on a cutting board, flatten it using a meat tenderizer. And use a meat tenderizer to flatten it.
3. Spread onion mix on pork, roll tight, cut into moderate rolls. Put them in your warm upped air fryer at 360 deg. F & cook them for 35 mins.
4. Present & relish!

PER SERVING

Calories: 304kcal	Fat: 10.2g	Carbs: 15g	Protein: 26.2g

CHAPTER 6: Meat

91. AIR-FRIED TURKEY BREAST

PREPARATION TIME	COOKING TIME	SERVING
10 mins	1 hr	8

INGREDIENTS	DIRECTIONS
• 1 tbsp. olive oil • 3–4 lbs. turkey breast, skin-on, bone-in, & thawed • 2 tsp. seasoning salt of choice	1. Set the air fryer to 350 deg. F. 2. Rub the oil over the turkey breast & thoroughly dust it using salt. 3. Organize the turkey in the fryer with its skin side down, about 20 mins. Continue cooking till it's done, about 30–40 mins. 4. It's done when the internal temp. reaches 165 deg. F/74 deg. C.

PER SERVING			
Calories: 263kcal	Fat: 10.1g	Carbs: 0.3g	Protein: 40.2g

92. CHICKEN TIKKA MASALA

PREPARATION TIME	COOKING TIME	SERVING
45 mins	10 mins	2

INGREDIENTS	DIRECTIONS
• 3 chicken breast fillets, chopped • 1 container tikka masala sauce	1. Marinate the chicken in the sauce for 30 mins. 2. Include the chicken to the air fryer. 3. Air-fry at 350 deg. F for 5 mins per side.

PER SERVING			
Calories: 403kcal	Fat: 25g	Carbs: 20.5g	Protein: 27.2g

93. BASIL CHICKEN

PREPARATION TIME	COOKING TIME	SERVING
15 mins	25 mins	4

INGREDIENTS	DIRECTIONS
• Pepper & salt • 2 tsp paprika, smoked • 0.5 tsp. basil, dried • 0.5 cup chicken stock • 0.5 lb. chicken breasts, cubed	1. Turn on the air fryer to 390 deg. F. 2. Bring out a pan & toss the components inside before putting it into the air fryer. 3. After 25 mins of baking, split this between a few plates & present with a side salad.

PER SERVING			
Calories: 221kcal	Fat: 11g	Carbs: 4.9g	Protein: 15g

94. GARLIC CHICKEN WINGS

PREPARATION TIME	COOKING TIME	SERVING
8 mins	30 mins	6

INGREDIENTS	DIRECTIONS
• 1 tsp of salt • 2 lbs. of chicken wings • 1 tsp of parsley • 2 tbsp of minced garlic • 1/4 tsp of pepper • 3/4 cup of Parmesan cheese, grated	1. Mix the entire components in a container. Mix wings in it. 2. Cook wings in the air fryer for about 28 mins at 400 deg. F. 3. Flip & cook for about 12 mins. Present with ketchup & relish.

PER SERVING			
Calories: 350kcal	Fat: 23g	Carbs: 11g	Protein: 37g

95. LOW-CARB FRIED CHICKEN

PREPARATION TIME	COOKING TIME	SERVING
10 mins	25 mins	4

INGREDIENTS	DIRECTIONS
• ¼ cup coconut flour • ¼ tsp. black pepper • half tsp. salt • 2 large eggs • 1 cup pork rinds • 1 tsp. smoked paprika • half tsp. garlic powder	1. Use 3 similar dishes to prepare the components to coat the chicken. 2. Beat the flour with the pepper & salt in a shallow container. 3. Break the eggs in a second shallow container & briskly beat. 4. Crush the pork rinds & mix with the garlic powder & paprika in the last container.

- 1 lb. chicken tenders, about 6 chicken drumsticks, thighs, & breasts

5. Immerse the pieces of chicken in the flour. Dip them into the egg, slightly shaking to remove any excess. Gently press it into the pork rind mixture to coat on the entire sides.

6. Allow the fryer unit to heat to 400 deg. F/204 deg. C for 5 mins.

7. Organize the prepared chicken in the basket (not stacked). Air-fry those till they're as crispy as desired, about 15–20 mins.

8. As you prepare them (in batches if needed), keep them in a container tented with a layer of foil in a low-temp. oven.

9. Present immediately for the most flavorful result.

PER SERVING			
Calories: 306kcal	Fat: 10.7g	Carbs: 1.5g	Protein: 49.3g

96. Chicken Fajitas

PREPARATION TIME	COOKING TIME	SERVING
10 mins	15 mins	8

INGREDIENTS	DIRECTIONS
<ul><li>2 (1 lb.) chicken breasts</li><li>1 red onion</li><li>1 fresh bell pepper, each green, yellow, & red</li><li>3 tbsp. fajita seasoning</li><li>1 tbsp. vegetable oil</li><li>Warmed tortillas, avocado slices, Pico de Gallo, or guacamole, for serving</li></ul>	1. Heat the air fryer to 390 deg. F/199 deg. C. 2. Discard the fat & bones from the chicken, & slice it into strips. 3. Slice the peppers into half-inch slices & the onion into wedges. 4. Drizzle the oil over the chicken strips, & season with the fajita seasoning. 5. Thoroughly toss them so they're evenly coated with the seasoning. 6. Scatter the veggies into the mixture, tossing gently till covered. 7. Organize the entire of the components in an air fryer basket. Air-fry for 15 mins, tossing halfway through the frying cycle. 8. Present with warmed tortillas, avocado slices, Pico de Gallo, or guacamole.

PER SERVING			
Calories: 154kcal	**Fat:** 10g	**Carbs:** 4g	**Protein:** 11g

97. CREAMY CHICKEN

PREPARATION TIME	COOKING TIME	SERVING
10 mins	20 mins	4

INGREDIENTS	DIRECTIONS
<ul><li>Pepper & salt</li><li>1 tsp. Olive oil</li><li>0.5 tsp. Sweet paprika</li><li>0.25 cup cream cheese</li><li>4 Chicken breasts, cubed</li></ul>	1. Turn on the air fryer to 370 deg. F. 2. Prepare a pan that fits into the machine with some oil before including the components inside. 3. Include this to the air fryer & let it bake. After 17 mins, you can split between the few plates & present!

PER SERVING			
Calories: 249kcal	**Fat:** 10g	**Carbs:** 5g	**Protein:** 18g

98. HONEY-LIME CHICKEN WINGS

PREPARATION TIME	COOKING TIME	SERVING
8 mins	30 mins	4

INGREDIENTS	DIRECTIONS
<ul><li>2 lbs. chicken wings</li><li>2 tbsp fresh lime juice</li><li>0.25 cup honey</li><li>1 tbsp. lime zest</li><li>1 garlic clove - pressed</li></ul>	1. Warm up the Air Fryer at 360 deg. F. 2. Beat the honey, lime juice, garlic & zest. Cover the wings with the mixture. 3. Cook for 25-30 mins till crispy. Shake the basket every 8 mins. Present & relish.

PER SERVING			
Calories: 114kcal	**Fat:** 0.9g	**Carbs:** 21g	**Protein:** 5g

99. CHICKEN HASH

PREPARATION TIME	COOKING TIME	SERVING

4 mins	10 mins	3

INGREDIENTS	DIRECTIONS
<ul><li>6 oz. cauliflower</li><li>7 oz. chicken fillet</li><li>half yellow onion</li><li>1 green pepper</li><li>1 tbsp. cream</li><li>1 tsp. black pepper</li></ul>	1. Heat the air fryer to 380 deg. F/194 deg. C. 2. Chop the cauliflower & include it to a blender to make rice. 3. Dice the chicken into bite-sized chunks & dust using pepper & salt. 4. Dice the green pepper & onion. Combine the components. 5. Include the fryer basket, cook it till done (about 6–7 mins), & present.

PER SERVING

Calories: 261kcal	Fat: 16.8g	Carbs: 7.1g	Protein: 21g

100. PECAN CRUSTED CHICKEN

PREPARATION TIME	COOKING TIME	SERVING
10 mins	25 mins	6

INGREDIENTS	DIRECTIONS
<ul><li>6 chicken tenders</li><li>Kosher salt as required</li><li>Freshly ground black pepper as required</li><li>1 tbsp. paprika</li><li>2 tbsps. honey</li><li>1 tbsp. mustard</li><li>2 pecans</li></ul>	1. Put the chicken tenders in a container. Include pepper, salt, honey, mustard & smoked paprika. Mix well till the chicken is covered with the spices. 2. Put the finely chopped pecans on a plate. 3. Roll the tender into the shredded pecans, one chicken tender at a time, till both sides are covered. Brush off excess material. 4. Put the offers in the air fryer basket & continue till the entire offers have been coated & are in the air fryer basket. 5. Set the air fryer to 350 deg. F for 12 mins 'til the chicken is cooked through.

PER SERVING

Calories: 94kcal	Fat: 7.1g	Carbs: 2.9g	Protein: 5g

101.CHICKEN THIGHS

PREPARATION TIME	COOKING TIME	SERVING
10 mins	20 mins	4

INGREDIENTS

- 4 chicken thighs
- 2 tsp. olive oil
- half tsp. each black pepper & salt
- 1 tsp. smoked paprika
- ¾ tsp. garlic powder

DIRECTIONS

1. Set the air fryer to reach 400 deg. F/204 deg. C.
2. Remove the bones from the thighs, but leave them with the skin.
3. Pat the thighs dry using a few paper towels. Brush the skin with a spritz of oil.
4. Organize the chicken thighs skin-side down & single-layered on a plate.
5. Beat the paprika, salt, pepper, & garlic powder in a mixing container.
6. Sprinkle about half of the seasoning mixture evenly over the thighs. Turn the thighs over & evenly sprinkle the remaining seasoning mixture on top.
7. Put each of the thighs skin-side up in the fryer basket (not stacked).
8. Fry the chicken till it's brown then the juices run clear when poked with a fork, about 18 mins. The centermost part of the chicken should reach a minimum of 165 deg. F/74 deg. C.

PER SERVING

Calories: 213kcal	Fat: 4g	Carbs: 0.9g	Protein: 19.3g

102.KOREAN FRIED CHICKEN

PREPARATION TIME	COOKING TIME	SERVING
10 mins	12 mins	4

INGREDIENTS

- half cup flour
- Salt & pepper, as required
- half cup water
- 1 lb. chicken
- 1 tbsp. sugar
- 3 tsp. chili garlic paste

DIRECTIONS

1. Mix the flour, salt, pepper, & water.
2. Coat the chicken with the batter.
3. Air-fry at 350 deg. F for 5 to 8 mins.
4. In a container, mix the remaining components.
5. Toss the chicken in the sauce.

- 1 tbsp. cider vinegar

6. Air-fry at 370 deg. F for 4 mins.

PER SERVING

| Calories: 472kcal | Fat: 23.8g | Carbs: 44.4g | Protein: 18.6g |

103. CHICKEN PAPRIKA

PREPARATION TIME	COOKING TIME	SERVING
15 mins	30 mins	4

INGREDIENTS	DIRECTIONS
<ul><li>1 lb. chicken wings</li><li>Olive oil, as needed</li><li>Salt & pepper, as required</li><li>1 tsp. garlic powder</li><li>3 tsp. smoked paprika</li></ul>	1. Drizzle the chicken wings with olive oil. 2. Season with the salt, pepper, garlic powder, & smoked paprika. 3. Air-fry at 400 deg. F for 30 mins, turning once or twice.

PER SERVING

| Calories: 170kcal | Fat: 9.8g | Carbs: 7.8g | Protein: 13g |

104. TURKEY MEATBALLS

PREPARATION TIME	COOKING TIME	SERVING
5 mins	20 mins	4

INGREDIENTS	DIRECTIONS
<ul><li>1.5 lbs. ground turkey</li><li>1/4 cup parsley</li><li>1 cup Panko bread crumbs</li><li>1 egg</li><li>1 tbsp low sodium soy sauce</li><li>Ground black pepper</li></ul>	1. First, in a container mix the components. 2. Create meatballs. 3. Oil the basket of the air fryer then put the patties in it. 4. Cook at 400 deg. F for ten mins. Turn the meatballs halfway through cooking. 5. Present & relish!

PER SERVING

| Calories: 160kcal | Fat: 2.7g | Carbs: 5g | Protein: 30g |

105. CHICKEN KEBABS

PREPARATION TIME	COOKING TIME	SERVING
10 mins	20 mins	2

INGREDIENTS

- 1/4 cup of honey
- Cooking spray
- 1/3 cup of soy sauce
- 6 mushrooms, chopped
- 3 bell peppers, chopped
- 2 chicken breasts, chopped
- Salt & black pepper, as per taste

DIRECTIONS

1. Combine the chicken, salt, honey, pepper, soy sauce, & oil in a large mixing container.
2. Mash everything together with mushrooms & bell peppers.
3. Make kebabs & air fry for about 20 mins at 338 deg. F. Present & relish

PER SERVING

Calories: 261kcal	Fat: 7g	Carbs: 12g	Protein: 6g

CHAPTER 7: Fish

106.MONKFISH WITH OLIVES & CAPERS

PREPARATION TIME	COOKING TIME	SERVING
5 mins	40 mins	4

INGREDIENTS

- 1 monkfish
- 10 cherry tomatoes
- 1/3 cup olives
- 5 capers
- Oil
- Salt

DIRECTIONS

1. Spread aluminum foil inside the air fryer basket & put the monkfish clean & skinless.
2. Include chopped tomatoes, olives, capers, oil, & salt.
3. Set the temp. to 160 deg. C (320 deg. F).
4. Cook the monkfish for about 40 mins.

PER SERVING

Calories: 404kcal	Fat: 29g	Carbs: 36g	Protein: 24g

107.SPLENDID SALMON PATTIES

PREPARATION TIME	COOKING TIME	SERVING
10 mins	15 mins	2

INGREDIENTS

- 1 (14-oz.) can salmon, canned & drained
- ¼ cup onion, chopped
- ¼ cup ground oats
- ¼ cup wheat flour
- 1 egg
- ¼ cup mayonnaise
- 1 tbsp. parsley
- 1 tsp. salt
- 1 tsp. black pepper
- 1 cup breadcrumbs

DIRECTIONS

1. First, warm up the Air Fryer to 390 deg. F.
2. Using a container, include & mix the canned salmon, onion, ground oats, wheat flour, egg, parsley, salt, black pepper, & the mayonnaise properly.
3. Split the salmon mixture into 4 patties & cover it with the breadcrumbs.
4. Include the salmon patties inside your air fryer then cook it for 8 to 10 mins or till it has a golden-brown color.
5. Present & relish!

PER SERVING

Calories: 260kcal	Fat: 15g	Carbs: 14g	Protein: 16g

108.LEMON TUNA

PREPARATION TIME	COOKING TIME	SERVING
10 mins	12 mins	4

INGREDIENTS	DIRECTIONS
• 1 tbsp. fresh lime juice • 1 egg • 3 tbsps. canola oil • 2 tbsps. hot sauce • 2 tsps. Dijon mustard • 2 tbsps. fresh parsley, chopped • half lb. plain tuna, water packed • half cup breadcrumbs • Salt & ground black pepper	1. Include tuna fish, parsley, mustard, crumbs, citrus juice, & hot sauce in a container. Mix well. Now, include oil, salt, & eggs in the container & make patties from the mixture. Refrigerate. 2. Warm up your Air Fryer to 360 deg. F. 3. Put the patties in the basket & cook for twelve mins. 4. Present & relish.

PER SERVING			
Calories: 315kcal	Fat: 18.7g	Carbs: 25g	Protein: 10.7g

109.SHRIMP, ZUCCHINI & CHERRY TOMATO SAUCE

PREPARATION TIME	COOKING TIME	SERVING
5 mins	30 mins	4

INGREDIENTS	DIRECTIONS
• 2 zucchinis • 1 cup shrimp • 7 cherry tomatoes • Salt & pepper as required • 1 clove garlic	1. Pour the oil into the air fryer, & include the garlic clove & chopped zucchini. 2. Cook for 15 mins at 300 deg. F. 3. Include the shrimp & the pieces of tomato, salt, & spices. 4. Cook for another 5 to 10 mins or 'til the shrimp water evaporates.

PER SERVING			
Calories: 214.3kcal	Fat: 8.6g	Carbs: 7.8g	Protein: 27.0g

110.SPINACH WITH SALMON & SEASHELLS

PREPARATION TIME	COOKING TIME	SERVING
5 mins	10 mins	1

INGREDIENTS	DIRECTIONS
• 1 lb. seashells • 1 pack spinach (chopped) • 2 tbsp. oil • 7 cloves garlic (minced) • 1 lb. salmon (chopped) • 1 tsp. red pepper flakes • Salt for taste	1. Include oil into the air fryer pot. 2. Mix salt with tuna fish, garlic, red pepper flakes, spinach, & seashells. 3. Cook at 300 deg. F for 15 mins. 4. When the pot beeps, present & relish!

PER SERVING			
Calories: 100kcal	Fat: 10g	Carbs: 8g	Protein: 11.5g

111.BUTTERED SCALLOPS

PREPARATION TIME	COOKING TIME	SERVING
10 mins	5 mins	4

INGREDIENTS	DIRECTIONS
• 4 tbsps. butter, melted • 3-lbs. sea scallops • 2 tbsps. thyme, minced • Salt & ground black pepper, as required	1. Include butter, sea scallops, thyme, salt, & pepper in a container. Toss to coat well. 2. Warm up your Air Fryer to 385 deg. F, & oil the basket. 3. Put scallops in the basket & cook for 5 mins. 4. Present & relish.

PER SERVING			
Calories: 203kcal	Fat: 7.1g	Carbs: 4.5g	Protein: 28.7g

112.BASIL COD

PREPARATION TIME	COOKING TIME	SERVING
5 mins	10 mins	2

INGREDIENTS	DIRECTIONS
• 2 cod loin fillets • Thyme • 2 Tsp basil • Pepper • Parsley • Oregano • 150g cherry Tomatoes halved • Salt	1. In a container, season the cod fillets except with basil. 2. Put the fillets & cherry tomatoes in the air fryer. Finally, season with the basil. Cook for 10 mins at 360 deg. F. 3. Present & relish.

PER SERVING			
Calories: 655kcal	Fat: 6g	Carbs: 3.8g	Protein: 31.9g

113. CAJUN SPICED SALMON

PREPARATION TIME	COOKING TIME	SERVING
10 mins	8 mins	8

INGREDIENTS	DIRECTIONS
• 4 tbsps. Cajun seasoning • 4 salmon steaks	1. Include Cajun seasoning in a container & rub salmon evenly with it. 2. Warm up the air fryer to 385 deg. F. 3. Organize air fryer grill pan & put salmon steaks on it. 4. Cook for about 8 mins & flip once in the middle way. 5. Take out & present hot.

PER SERVING			
Calories: 218kcal	Fat: 5.5g	Carbs: 3.9g	Protein: 27.3g

114. SIMPLE SALMON

PREPARATION TIME	COOKING TIME	SERVING
10 mins	12 mins	2

INGREDIENTS	DIRECTIONS
• 2 (4-oz.) salmon fillets, skin removed • 1 moderate lemon. • 2 tbsps. butter, unsalted & melted.	1. Put each fillet on aluminum foil. Include the butter. Sprinkle dill, garlic powder, & lemon zest over salmon.

- half tsp. dill, dried
- half tsp. garlic powder.

2. Fold the aluminum foil & close completely & create packets. Put the foil packets in the basket of the air fryer. Bake for 12 mins at 400 deg. F.
3. Present warm.

PER SERVING			
Calories: 252kcal	Fat: 11g	Carbs: 2g	Protein: 29g

115. SEASONED CATFISH

PREPARATION TIME	COOKING TIME	SERVING
10 mins	14 mins	4

INGREDIENTS	DIRECTIONS
• ¼ cup seasoned fish fry • 1 tbsp olive oil • 4 (6-ounce) catfish fillets • Cooking Spray	1. Oil the basket with cooking spray & then warm up the air fryer to 400 deg. F for a few mins. 2. In a container, season the fillets with the seasoning & oil. 3. Put the fish fillets in the basket & cook for 13 mins. 4. Turn the fish fillets halfway through cooking. 5. Present & relish.

PER SERVING			
Calories: 202kcal	Fat: 9.4g	Carbs: 11.4g	Protein: 24.7g

116. GARLIC LEMON SHRIMP

PREPARATION TIME	COOKING TIME	SERVING
11 mins	6 mins	2

INGREDIENTS	DIRECTIONS
• 8 oz. moderate shrimp, shelled • 1 moderate lemon. • 2 tbsps. butter, melted. • half tsp. garlic, minced • half tsp. Old Bay seasoning	1. In a large container, squeeze lemon juice over shrimp. 2. Include remaining components & lemon zest & toss to combine. 3. Put the contents of the container in the basket of the air fryer. 4. Cook at 400 deg. F for 6 mins. 5. Present & relish.

PER SERVING			
Calories: 190kcal	**Fat:** 18g	**Carbs:** 9g	**Protein:** 14g

117. SHRIMP & GREEN BEANS

PREPARATION TIME	COOKING TIME	SERVING
10 mins	15 mins	4

INGREDIENTS

- half lb. green beans, trimmed & halved
- 1 lb. shrimp, skinned & deveined
- ¼ cup ghee, melted
- 2 tbsps. cilantro, chopped.
- Juice of 1 lime
- A tweak of salt & black pepper

DIRECTIONS

1. In a pan, mix the entire the components, & toss.
2. Warm up the Air Fryer.
3. Introduce in the Air fryer & cook at 360 deg. F for 15 mins.
4. Shaking the fryer halfway.
5. Present & relish!

PER SERVING			
Calories: 222kcal	**Fat:** 8g	**Carbs:** 5g	**Protein:** 10g

118. SOUTHERN-AIR-FRIED CATFISH

PREPARATION TIME	COOKING TIME	SERVING
10 mins	15 mins	4

INGREDIENTS

- 4 catfish fillets, skinless
- 1 tsp. salt
- 1 tsp. black pepper
- 1 cup cornmeal
- 1 cup flour

DIRECTIONS

1. Warm up your air fryer to 360 deg. F.
2. Using a container, include the cornmeal, flour, salt, & black pepper & mix it properly.
3. Dredge the catfish fillets in the seasoned cornmeal mixture.
4. Oil your air fryer with a non-stick cooking spray & include the catfish fillets.
5. Cook the catfish for 8 mins at a 360 deg. F or till it turns brown.
6. Present & relish!

PER SERVING			
Calories: 350kcal	**Fat:** 11g	**Carbs:** 31g	**Protein:** 25g

119. COD FISH NUGGETS

PREPARATION TIME	COOKING TIME	SERVING
5 mins	20 mins	4

INGREDIENTS

- 1 lb. COD fillet
- 3 eggs
- 4 tbsp. olive oil
- 1 cup almond flour
- 1 cup gluten-free breadcrumbs

DIRECTIONS

1. Warm the Air Fryer to 390 deg. Fahrenheit.
2. Slice the cod into nuggets.
3. Prepare three containers. Beat the eggs in one. Combine the salt, oil, & breadcrumbs in another. Sift the almond flour into the third one.
4. Cover each nugget with flour, & dip in the eggs & the breadcrumbs.
5. Organize the nuggets in the basket & set the timer for 20 mins.
6. Present the fish with your favorite dips or sides.

PER SERVING

Calories: 334kcal	Fat: 10g	Carbs: 8g	Protein: 32g

120. CABBAGE WITH SALMON FISH

PREPARATION TIME	COOKING TIME	SERVING
6 mins	15 mins	1

INGREDIENTS

- half tsp. sesame oil
- 1 tbsp. canola oil
- 2 tbsp. Chile paste
- 2 cloves garlic (chopped)
- 4 Salmon fish (cubes)
- half cup soy sauce
- 1 onion (sliced)
- half cabbage (chopped)
- 2 carrots (chopped)
- 8 oz. noodles (cooked)

DIRECTIONS

1. Include sesame oil & canola oil into the air fryer pot.
2. Mix garlic & salmon cubes.
3. Include onion, soy sauce, Chile paste, cabbage, & carrots.
4. Cook at 300 deg. F for 15 mins.
5. When ready, present with noodles.

PER SERVING

Calories: 90kcal	Fat: 8g	Carbs: 20g	Protein: 25g

CHAPTER 8: Desserts

121. RICOTTA CHEESECAKE

PREPARATION TIME	COOKING TIME	SERVING
15 mins	25 mins	8

INGREDIENTS

- 17.6 oz. Ricotta cheese
- 3 eggs
- ¾ cup sugar
- 3 tbsps. corn starch
- 1 tbsp. fresh lemon juice
- 2 tsps. vanilla extract
- 1 tsp. fresh lemon zest, finely grated

DIRECTIONS

1. In a large container, put the entire components & mix till well combined. Put the mixture into a baking pan.
2. Set the cooking time of your air fryer to 25 mins & the temp. at 320 deg. F.
3. Refrigerate overnight before serving.

PER SERVING

Calories: 197kcal	Fat: 6.6g	Carbs: 25.7g	Protein: 9.2g

122. ANGEL FOOD CAKE

PREPARATION TIME	COOKING TIME	SERVING
5 mins	30 mins	12

INGREDIENTS

- 1 cup powdered erythritol
- 1 tsp. strawberry extract
- 12 egg whites
- 2 tsps. cream of tartar

DIRECTIONS

1. Warm up the air fryer.
2. Blend the cream of tartar & egg whites. Use a hand mixer & beat till white & fluffy.
3. Include the rest of the components then beat for another min. Pour into a baking dish & put in the air fryer basket.
4. Cook for 30 mins at 400 deg. F.

PER SERVING

Calories: 65kcal	Fat: 5g	Carbs: 6.2g	Protein: 3.1g

123.APPLE TREAT WITH RAISINS

PREPARATION TIME	COOKING TIME	SERVING
15 mins	10 mins	4

INGREDIENTS	DIRECTIONS
• 4 apples, cored • 1 half oz. almonds • ¾ oz. raisins • 2 tbsps. sugar	1. Warm up the air fryer to 360 deg. F. 2. In a container, mix almonds, sugar, & raisins, & blend the mixture using a hand mixer. 3. Fill cored apples with the almond mixture. 4. Put the prepared apples in your air fryer basket & cook for 10 mins. Present with powdered sugar.

PER SERVING			
Calories: 188kcal	Fat: 4.3g	Carbs: 15.9g	Protein: 3.8g

124.AIR FRIED BANANA WITH SESAME SEEDS

PREPARATION TIME	COOKING TIME	SERVING
15 mins	10 mins	5

INGREDIENTS	DIRECTIONS
• half cups flour • 5 bananas, sliced • 1 tsp. salt • 3 tbsps. sesame seeds • 1 cup water • 2 eggs, beaten • 1 tsp. baking powder • half tbsp. sugar	1. Warm up the air fryer on bake function to 340 deg. F. 2. In a container, mix salt, flour, sesame seeds, baking powder, eggs, sugar, & water. 3. Coat sliced bananas with the flour mixture. Put the prepared slices in the air fryer basket. Cook for 10 mins. Present chilled.

PER SERVING			
Calories: 327kcal	Fat: 6.5g	Carbs: 27.3g	Protein: 9.7g

125.CHOCOLATE SOUFFLÉ

PREPARATION TIME	COOKING TIME	SERVING
7 mins	12 mins	2

INGREDIENTS

- 6 tbsp. almond flour
- half tsp. vanilla
- half tbsp. sweetener
- 2 separated eggs
- ¼ cups melted coconut oil
- 4 oz. semi-sweet chocolate, chopped

DIRECTIONS

1. Warm up the Smart Air Fryer Oven to 330 deg. F.
2. Brush the coconut oil & sweetener onto ramekins.
3. Melt the coconut oil & chocolate together.
4. Beat the egg yolks well, including vanilla & sweetener.
5. Stir in the flour, & ensure there are no lumps.
6. Beat the egg whites till they reach peak state, & fold them into the chocolate mixture.
7. Pour the batter into ramekins, then put them into the Smart Air Fryer Oven & cook for 12 mins.
8. Present with powdered sugar dusted on top.

PER SERVING

Calories: 378kcal	Fat: 9g	Carbs: 5g	Protein: 4g

126. BAKED APPLES

PREPARATION TIME	COOKING TIME	SERVING
5 mins	15 mins	2

INGREDIENTS

- 2 apples
- 1 tsp butter, melted
- half tsp cinnamon

Topping Ingredients:

- ⅓ cup Old Fashioned / Rolled Oats
- 1 tbsp Butter, melted
- 1 tbsp Maple Syrup
- 1 tsp whole wheat flour
- half tsp cinnamon

DIRECTIONS

1. Cut the apples in half then remove the core, stem & seeds.
2. Brush butter over the sides of the apples & sprinkle half teaspoon cinnamon on top.
3. In a small container, mix together the topping components & disperse over the apples.
4. Carefully put the apple halves in the basket of the air fryer, then bake at 350 deg. F for 15 mins.

PER SERVING

Calories: 246kcal	Fat: 8g	Carbs: 42g	Protein: 4g

127. CHOCOLATE & POMEGRANATE BARS

PREPARATION TIME	COOKING TIME	SERVING
2 hrs 10 mins	4 mins	6

INGREDIENTS	DIRECTIONS
<ul><li>half cup milk</li><li>1 tbsp. vanilla extract</li><li>1 & half cups dark chocolate</li><li>half cup almonds</li><li>half cup pomegranate seeds</li></ul>	1. Warm pan with milk over moderate heat, put chocolate, turn for 5 mins, remove heat, put half of the pomegranate seeds, vanilla extract, & half of the nuts, & turn. 2. Put the mix into a lined baking pan, spray, disperse a tweak salt, nuts, & remaining pomegranate, get in air fryer & cook at 300 deg. F for 4 mins. 3. Allow into the fridge for 2 hrs, then present.

PER SERVING			
Calories: 139kcal	Fat: 8.17g	Carbs: 13.3g	Protein: 2.37g

128. APPLE HAND PIES

PREPARATION TIME	COOKING TIME	SERVING
5 mins	8 mins	6

INGREDIENTS	DIRECTIONS
<ul><li>15-ounces no-sugar-included apple pie filling</li><li>1 store-bought crust</li></ul>	1. Lay out the pie crust & slice it into equal-sized squares. 2. Put 2 tbsp. filling into each square & sealing the crust with a fork. 3. Pour into the Oven rack/basket. Put the Rack on the middle shelf of the Air fryer oven. 4. Set temp. to 390 deg. F, & set time to 8 mins till golden in color.

PER SERVING			
Calories: 278kcal	Fat: 10g	Carbs: 17g	Protein: 5g

129. BERRY YOGURT CAKE

PREPARATION TIME	COOKING TIME	SERVING
15 mins	60 mins	12

INGREDIENTS	DIRECTIONS
<ul><li>2 eggs</li><li>1 lemon</li><li>1 cup of berries</li><li>half tsp of salt</li><li>1 half tsp of baking powder</li><li>1 half cups of cake flour</li><li>1/4 tsp of baking soda</li><li>1 cup of brown sugar</li><li>half tsp of vanilla extract</li><li>half cup of olive oil</li><li>half cup of Greek yogurt</li><li>3 tbsp of lemon juice</li></ul>	1. Include the entire the components except baking powder, soda, salt, & flour to a separate container & beat together till smooth. 2. Then combine the salt, baking powder, soda, & flour. 3. Include olive oil & beat till well combined. 4. Include mixed berries. Warm up the air fryer to 300 deg. F. 5. Oil pan with oil. Include the batter to it. 6. Cook in the air fryer for about 60 mins. 7. Then, slice & present.

PER SERVING			
Calories: 291kcal	Fat: 10g	Carbs: 44g	Protein: 5g

130. COCOA & ALMOND BARS

PREPARATION TIME	COOKING TIME	SERVING
34 mins	4 mins	6

INGREDIENTS	DIRECTIONS
<ul><li>¼ cup cocoa nibs</li><li>1 cup almonds</li><li>2 tbsps. Cocoa powder</li><li>¼ cup hemp seeds</li><li>¼ cup goji berries</li><li>¼ cup coconut</li><li>8 dates</li></ul>	1. Blend almonds in the food processor, put hemp seeds, cocoa powder, cocoa nibs, coconut, goji, & beat properly. 2. Put dates, beat properly. Spray on a lined baking sheet & get in the air fryer. Cook at 320 deg. F for 4 mins. 3. Slice & allow in the fridge for 30 mins.

PER SERVING			
Calories: 96kcal	Fat: 3g	Carbs: 22g	Protein: 8.5g

131. APPLE DUMPLINGS

PREPARATION TIME	COOKING TIME	SERVING
10 mins	25 mins	4

INGREDIENTS

- 2 tbsp. melted coconut oil
- 2 puff pastry sheets
- 1 tbsp. brown sugar
- 2 tbsp. raisins
- 2 small apples of choice

DIRECTIONS

1. Ensure your air fryer oven is warm upped to 356 degrees.
2. Core & peel apples & mix with raisins & sugar.
3. Put a bit of apple mixture into puff pastry sheets & brush the sides with melted coconut oil.
4. Put into the air fryer. Cook for 25 mins, turning halfway through. It will be golden when done.

PER SERVING

Calories: 367kcal	Fat: 7g	Carbs: 10g	Protein: 2g

132. CHOCOLATE MUG CAKE

PREPARATION TIME	COOKING TIME	SERVING
7 mins	18 mins	3

INGREDIENTS

- half cup cocoa powder
- half cup stevia powder
- 1 cup coconut cream
- 1 package cream cheese, at room temp.
- 1 tbsp. vanilla extract
- 1 tbsp. butter

DIRECTIONS

1. Warm up the Smart Air Fryer Oven at 350 deg. F for 5 mins.
2. In a mixing container, combine the entire the listed components using a hand mixer till fluffy.
3. Pour the mixture into the oiled mugs.
4. Put the mugs in the fryer basket & bake at 350 deg. F for 13 mins.
5. Present when cool.

PER SERVING

Calories: 100kcal	Fat: 0g	Carbs: 21g	Protein: 3g

133. GLAZED BANANAS

PREPARATION TIME	COOKING TIME	SERVING
10 mins	10 mins	2

INGREDIENTS

- 1 ripe banana, skinned & sliced
- half tsp. fresh lime juice

DIRECTIONS

1. Coat each banana half with lime juice.

- 2 tsps. maple syrup
- ¼ tsp. ground cinnamon

2. Organize the banana halves onto the oiled sheet pan, cut sides up.
3. Drizzle the banana halves with maple syrup & sprinkle with cinnamon.
4. Organize the baking dish in your air fryer. Set the temp. to 350 deg. F & the timer for 10 mins.

PER SERVING

Calories: 70kcal	Fat: 0.2g	Carbs: 18.1g	Protein: 0.7g

134. BLUEBERRY PUDDING

PREPARATION TIME	COOKING TIME	SERVING
5 mins	25 mins	6

INGREDIENTS	DIRECTIONS
<ul><li>2 cups flour</li><li>2 cups rolled oats</li><li>8 cups blueberries</li><li>1 stick margarine</li><li>1 cup walnuts</li><li>3 tbsps. Maple syrup</li><li>2 tbsps. Rosemary</li></ul>	1. Spray blueberries smeared baking pan & keep. 2. Mix rolled oats with walnuts, flour, margarine, rosemary, & maple syrup, beat properly, put mix over blueberries, put the entire in the air fryer & cook at 350 deg. F for 25 mins. 3. Allow to cool, slice. Present.

PER SERVING

Calories: 278kcal	Fat: 17g	Carbs: 26.5g	Protein: 14g

135. AIR FRIED APPLES

PREPARATION TIME	COOKING TIME	SERVING
10 mins	17 mins	4

INGREDIENTS	DIRECTIONS
<ul><li>4 big apples</li><li>A handful raisins</li><li>1 tbsp. cinnamon</li><li>Raw honey</li></ul>	1. Infuse each apple with raisins, spray cinnamon, sprinkle honey. 2. Put them into the air fryer, & cook at 367 deg. F for 17 mins. 3. Allow to cool. Present.

PER SERVING

Calories: 110kcal	Fat: 0.3g	Carbs: 26.8g	Protein: 4.5g

136. CHOCOLATE CAKE

PREPARATION TIME	COOKING TIME	SERVING
6 mins	35 mins	9

INGREDIENTS

- half cups hot water
- 1 tsp. vanilla
- ¼ cups olive oil
- half cups almond milk
- 1 egg
- half tsp. salt
- ¾ tsp. baking soda
- ¾ tsp. baking powder
- half cups unsweetened cocoa powder
- 2 cups almond flour
- 1 cup brown sugar

DIRECTIONS

1. Warm up your Smart Air Fryer Oven to 356 deg. F.
2. Stir the entire the dry components together, then stir in the wet components.
3. Include the hot water. (The batter should be thin.)
4. Pour the cake batter into a pan that fits into the fryer.
5. Bake for 35 mins.

PER SERVING

Calories: 378kcal	Fat: 9g	Carbs: 5g	Protein: 4g

137. CHERRY-CHOCO BARS

PREPARATION TIME	COOKING TIME	SERVING
7 mins	15 mins	8

INGREDIENTS

- ¼ tsp. salt
- half cup almonds, sliced
- half cup chia seeds
- half cup dark chocolate, chopped
- half cup dried cherries, chopped
- half cup prunes, puréed
- half cup quinoa, cooked
- ¾ cup almond butter
- 1/3 cup honey
- half cups oats
- 2 tbsp. coconut oil

DIRECTIONS

1. Warm up the Smart Air Fryer Oven to 375 deg. F.
2. In a container, combine the oats, quinoa, chia seeds, almond, cherries, & chocolate.
3. In a saucepan, heat the almond butter, honey, & coconut oil.
4. Pour the butter mixture over the dry mixture, then include the salt & prunes, & mix till well combined.
5. Pour this over a baking dish that can fit inside the air fryer.
6. Bake for 15 mins.
7. Let it cool before slicing it into bars.

PER SERVING

| Calories: 378kcal | Fat: 9g | Carbs: 5g | Protein: 4g |

138. BERRIES MIX

PREPARATION TIME	COOKING TIME	SERVING
11 mins	6 mins	4

INGREDIENTS

- 2 tbsp. lemon juice
- 1-half tbsps. maple syrup
- 1-half tbsps. champagne vinegar
- 1 tbsp. Olive oil
- 1 lb. strawberries
- 1-half cups blueberries
- ¼ cup basil leaves

DIRECTIONS

1. Mix in lemon juice with vinegar & maple syrup in a pan, boil over moderate heat. Put oil, strawberries, & blueberries.
2. Put the mix in the air fryer & cook at 310 deg. F for 6 mins.
3. Dust basil over, then present.

PER SERVING

| Calories: 138kcal | Fat: 3.9g | Carbs: 23.4g | Protein: 1.21g |

139. CARROT CAKE

PREPARATION TIME	COOKING TIME	SERVING
11 mins	6 mins	4

INGREDIENTS

- 5 oz. flour
- ¾ tbsp. baking powder
- half tbsp. baking soda
- half tbsp. cinnamon powder
- ¼ tbsp. nutmeg
- half tbsp. the entire spice
- 1 egg
- 3 tbsps. yogurt
- half cup sugar
- ¼ cup pineapple juice
- 4 tbsps. sunflower oil
- ⅓ cup carrots
- ⅓ cup pecans

DIRECTIONS

1. Mix flour with baking powder, salt, baking soda, allspice, nutmeg, & cinnamon in a container, then turn.
2. Mix egg with yogurt, oil, sugar, pineapple juice, carrots, coconut flakes, & pecans in another container, then turn properly.
3. Blend the two mixtures & turn properly, put the mix into a spring form pan smeared with some cooking spray, get it into the air fryer, then cook at 320 deg. F for 45 mins.
4. Allow to cool, then slice. Present.

- ⅓ cup coconut flakes
- Cooking spray

PER SERVING

Calories: 301kcal	Fat: 16.8g	Carbs: 30g	Protein: 7g

140.BLUEBERRY LEMON MUFFINS

PREPARATION TIME	COOKING TIME	SERVING
7 mins	8 mins	12

INGREDIENTS	DIRECTIONS
<ul><li>1 tsp. vanilla</li><li>1 lemon, juiced & zested</li><li>3 eggs</li><li>half cups cream</li><li>¼ cups avocado oil</li><li>half cup monk fruit</li><li>2 half cups almond flour</li></ul>	1. Mix the monk fruit & flour. 2. In another container, mix the vanilla, egg, lemon juice, & cream. 3. Put the mixtures together & blend well. 4. Spoon the batter into cupcake holders. 5. Put in the Smart Air Fryer Oven, then bake at 320 deg. F for 8 mins, checking at 6 mins to ensure you don't overbake them.

PER SERVING

Calories: 378kcal	Fat: 9g	Carbs: 5g	Protein: 4g

CHAPTER 9: Liquids

141. *HEALTHY BEAN SOUP*

PREPARATION TIME	COOKING TIME	SERVING
30 mins	20 mins	10

INGREDIENTS	DIRECTIONS
<ul><li>Handful of cilantro</li><li>3 tsp of cumin</li><li>4 tomatoes, chopped</li><li>half cup of water</li><li>3/4 tsp of sea salt</li><li>2 jalapenos, chopped</li><li>4 cans of black beans</li><li>1/4 cup of lime juice</li><li>half cup of onion, chopped</li><li>2 cups of vegetable broth</li><li>1/4 cup of cilantro, chopped</li></ul>	1. Mix the entire the veggies & spices in a container. Keep in the fridge for about 30 mins. 2. Include beans, vegetable broth, cumin, & water to a ramekin. 3. Cook for about 10 mins at 400 deg. F. 4. Also, air fry veggies. Mix everything & cook for 5 mins. 5. Top with cilantro & present.

PER SERVING			
Calories: 250kcal	Fat: 8g	Carbs: 44g	Protein: 9g

142. *ONION SOUP*

PREPARATION TIME	COOKING TIME	SERVING
5 mins	1 hr	4

INGREDIENTS	DIRECTIONS
<ul><li>6 cups beef stock</li><li>3 tbsps butter</li><li>1 bay leaf</li><li>6 cups, sliced onions</li><li>half teaspoon salt</li><li>1 teaspoon soy sauce</li><li>2 teaspoons thyme</li></ul>	1. Line the basket with aluminum foil & heat the air fryer to 300 deg. F. Cook onions for 30 mins, stirring often. 2. In a saucepan over moderate heat, cook for 15 min the onions, thyme, butter, soy, & salt. Also, include the bay leaf. 3. Pour in the beef broth & then simmer for 15 min. 4. Remove the bay leaf & blend everything. 5. Present in soup containers.

PER SERVING			
Calories: 268kcal	Fat: 8g	Carbs: 25g	Protein: 10g

143. ASIAN PORK SOUP

PREPARATION TIME	COOKING TIME	SERVING
10 mins	30 mins	5

INGREDIENTS	DIRECTIONS
<ul><li>1 lb. ground pork</li><li>1 tsp. ground ginger</li><li>¼ cup soy sauce</li><li>4 cups beef broth</li><li>half cabbage head, chopped</li><li>2 carrots, skinned & shredded</li><li>1 onion, chopped</li><li>1 tbsp. olive oil</li><li>Pepper</li><li>Salt</li></ul>	1. Include oil into the air fryer & set on Sauté mode. 2. Include meat to the pot & sauté for 5 mins. 3. Include remaining components & stir well. 4. Secure pot with lid & cooks on manual high pressure for 25 mins. 5. Quick release pressure, then opens the lid. 6. Stir well & present hot.

PER SERVING			
Calories: 229kcal	Fat: 7.2g	Carbs: 10.6g	Protein: 29.8g

144. BASIL TOMATO SOUP

PREPARATION TIME	COOKING TIME	SERVING
5 mins	15 mins	4

INGREDIENTS	DIRECTIONS
<ul><li>1 onion, roughly sliced</li><li>1 potato, roughly chopped</li><li>half cup of tomatoes</li><li>2 tbsps of tomato paste</li><li>2 tbsps of sun-dried tomatoes</li><li>1 tbsp of basil leaves, freshly chopped</li><li>1 carrot, roughly chopped</li><li>4 cups of water</li><li>Salt & black pepper as required</li><li>2 tbsps of butter</li></ul>	1. Set the Air fryer to 375 deg. F for 5 mins. Put the tomatoes, potato, carrot, & sun-dried tomatoes in the cooking tray. Insert the cooking tray into the Oven when it displays "Include Food." 2. Remove from the Oven when cooking time is complete. Put the butter in a wok & include the tomato mixture & onions. 3. Sauté it for about 3 mins, stirring the remaining components. Secure the wok's lid & cook for about 12 mins on moderate

heat. Puree the contents of the soup with an immersion blender & present hot.

PER SERVING

Calories: 239kcal	Fat: 12.8g	Carbs: 29.6g	Protein: 4.2g

145. ROASTED TOMATO SOUP

PREPARATION TIME	COOKING TIME	SERVING
15 mins	30 mins	6

INGREDIENTS	DIRECTIONS
• 6 fresh, halved tomatoes • 1 quartered white onion • 5 cloves, skinned garlic • 1 tbsp olive oil • half teaspoon pepper • 1 teaspoon granulated sugar • ¼ cup, chopped basil • 1half cups chicken broth • Salt & pepper as required	1. Heat the fryer to 400 deg. Include the onions, tomatoes, olive oil, salt, garlic, pepper, & sugar to the basket lined with baking paper. 2. Air fry for 30 mins till the vegetables are soft. Remember to peel the tomatoes & remove the stems once the vegetables are cooled. 3. Blend the vegetables in a food processor. Include the basil as well. 4. Transfer the vegetable soup to a pot. Pour in the chicken broth & heat. 5. Present hot!

PER SERVING

Calories: 198kcal	Fat: 7g	Carbs: 46g	Protein: 19g

146. AIR FRYER BEAN SOUP

PREPARATION TIME	COOKING TIME	SERVING
20 mins	1 hr and 25 mins	6

INGREDIENTS	DIRECTIONS
• 1 pound of white beans • 1 ¼ pound of beef shanks with bone • 1 white onion, chopped • 1 green bell pepper, chopped • 2 carrots, chopped • 4 tbsps olive oil • 2 tbsps fresh parsley, chopped	1. Immerse beans in a container of cold water overnight. 2. Put the beef shanks & olive oil in the air fryer & turn on fry setting. Brown on both sides 3. Remove the beans from the water, & rinse. Include beans, chopped tomatoes, paprika, bay leaves, & garlic.

- half teaspoon garlic, minced
- half tbsp salt
- 1 can of tomatoes, chopped
- 1-liter water
- 3 bay leaves
- half teaspoon paprika

4. Include water, close the lid, & cook on the manual high setting for 1 hr. Make sure the beans are soft, & if not, cook for another 30 mins. Present.

PER SERVING

Calories: 86kcal	Fat: 5g	Carbs: 9.7g	Protein: 2.8g

147. CHICKEN RICE NOODLE SOUP

PREPARATION TIME	COOKING TIME	SERVING
5 mins	10 mins	6

INGREDIENTS	DIRECTIONS
<ul><li>6 cups chicken, cooked & cubed</li><li>3 tbsp. rice vinegar</li><li>2 half cups cabbage, shredded</li><li>2 tbsp. fresh ginger, grated</li><li>2 tbsp. soy sauce</li><li>3 garlic cloves, minced</li><li>8 oz. rice noodles</li><li>1 bell pepper, chopped</li><li>1 large carrot, skinned & sliced</li><li>6 cups chicken stock</li><li>1 onion, chopped</li><li>half tsp. black pepper</li></ul>	1. Include the entire components into the air fryer & stir well. 2. Secure pot with lid & cooks on manual high pressure for 10 mins. 3. Quick release pressure, then opens the lid. 4. Stir well & present.

PER SERVING

Calories: 306kcal	Fat: 5.1g	Carbs: 18.7g	Protein: 43.1g

148. COCONUT LIME SOUP

PREPARATION TIME	COOKING TIME	SERVING
6 mins	10 mins	3-4

INGREDIENTS	DIRECTIONS
• half tbsp of coconut oil • 1 finely chopped onion • 1 tsp of ground coriander powder • 1 moderate sized cauliflower that is broken into a large floret • 3 cups of vegetable broth • half cup of coconut milk • 2-3 tbsp of lime juice • 1 tweak of salt as required	1. Start by heating the Air fryer & setting the Manual button to sauté mode, & sauté the onion for 6 mins. 2. Include the coriander & keep stirring for a couple of mins. 3. Include the rest of the components from the cauliflower, the vegetable broth, & the coconut milk; then, stir the components to combine them. 4. Set the timer to 10 mins. 5. Once the timer sets off; press the button, keep warm, & release the pressure 6. Blend the components with a blender till it becomes soft 7. Include the lime juice & adjust the salt as required 8. Present & relish your soup!

PER SERVING

Calories: 262.8kcal	Fat: 12.7g	Carbs: 16g	Protein: 22g

149. KALE BEEF SOUP

PREPARATION TIME	COOKING TIME	SERVING
15 mins	43 mins	4

INGREDIENTS	DIRECTIONS
• 1 lb. beef stew meat • 1 tsp. cayenne pepper • 3 garlic cloves, crushed • 4 cups chicken broth • 2 tbsp. olive oil • 1 cup kale, chopped • 1 onion, sliced • ¼ tsp. black pepper • half tsp. salt	1. Include oil into the air fryer & set on Sauté mode. 2. Include garlic & onion. Sauté for 3 mins. 3. Include meat & sauté for 5 mins. 4. Include broth & season with cayenne pepper, pepper, & salt. Stir well. 5. Secure pot with lid & cooks on manual high pressure for 25 mins. 6. Quick release pressure, then opens the lid. 7. Include kale & stir well. Sit for 10 mins. 8. Stir well & present.

PER SERVING

Calories: 333kcal	Fat: 15.6g	Carbs: 6.3g	Protein: 40.3g

150. CORN SOUP

PREPARATION TIME	COOKING TIME	SERVING
10 mins	15 mins	2

INGREDIENTS

- 2 leeks, chopped
- 2 tbsps butter
- 2 garlic cloves, skinned & minced
- 6 ears of corn, cobs represented, kernels cut off,
- 2 bay leaves
- 4 tarragon sprigs, chopped
- 1- quart chicken stock
- Salt & ground black pepper, as required
- Extra virgin olive oil
- 1 tbsp fresh chives, chopped

DIRECTIONS

1. Put the air fryer on Sauté mode, include the butter & melt it.
2. Include the leeks & garlic, stir, & cook for 4 mins. Include the corn, corn cobs, bay leaves, tarragon, & stock to cover everything, cover the Air fryer & cook on the Soup setting for 15 mins.
3. Release the pressure, uncover the Air fryer, discard the bay leaves & corn cobs, & transfer everything to a blender.
4. Pulse well to obtain a smooth soup, include the rest of the stock & blend again.
5. Include the salt & pepper, stir well, split into soup containers, & present cold with chives & olive oil on top.

PER SERVING

Calories: 300kcal	Fat: 8.3g	Carbs: 32g	Protein: 13g

Conversion Chart

Volume Equivalents (Liquid)

US Standard	US Standard (ounces)	Metric (approximate)
2 tbsps	1 fl. oz.	30 mL
¼ cup	2 fl. oz.	60 mL
half cup	4 fl. oz.	120 mL
1 cup	8 fl. oz.	240 mL
1half cups	12 fl. oz.	355 mL
2 cups or 1 pint	16 fl. oz.	475 mL
4 cups or 1 quart	32 fl. oz.	1 L
1 gallon	128 fl. oz.	4 L

Volume Equivalents (Dry)

US Standard	Metric (approximate)
⅛ teaspoon	0.5 mL
¼ teaspoon	1 mL
half teaspoon	2 mL
¾ teaspoon	4 mL
1 teaspoon	5 mL
1 tbsp	15 mL
¼ cup	59 mL
⅓ cup	79 mL
half cup	118 mL
⅔ cup	156 mL
¾ cup	177 mL
1 cup	235 mL
2 cups or 1 pint	475 mL
3 cups	700 mL
4 cups or 1 quart	1 L

Oven Temperatures

Fahrenheit (F)	Celsius (C) (approximate)
250°F	120°C
300°F	150°C
325°F	165°C
350°F	180°C
375°F	190°C

400°F	200°C
425°F	220°C
450°F	230°C

Weight Equivalents

US Standard	Metric (approximate)
1 tbsp	15 g
half ounce	15 g
1 ounce	30 g
2 ounces	60 g
4 ounces	115 g
8 ounces	225 g
12 ounces	340 g
16 ounces or 1 pound	455 g

30-Day Meal Plan

Days	Breakfast	Lunch	Dinner	Dessert
1	Onion Soup	Asian Pork Soup	Chicken Rice Noodle Soup	-
2	Healthy Bean Soup	Roasted Tomato Soup	Kale Beef Soup	-
3	Air Fryer Bean Soup	Coconut Lime Soup	Chicken Rice Noodle Soup	-
4	Asian Pork Soup	Basil Tomato Soup	Onion Soup	-
5	Kale Beef Soup	Air Fryer Bean Soup	Corn Soup	-
6	Roasted Tomato Soup	Healthy Bean Soup	Chicken Rice Noodle Soup	-
7	Basil Tomato Soup	Kale Beef Soup	Coconut Lime Soup	-
8	Coconut Lime Soup	Asian Pork Soup	Roasted Tomato Soup	-
9	Corn Soup	Healthy Bean Soup	Onion Soup	-
10	Chicken Rice Noodle Soup	Air Fryer Bean Soup	Corn Soup	-
11	Roasted Tomato Soup	Coconut Lime Soup	Basil Tomato Soup	-
12	Asian Pork Soup	Basil Tomato Soup	Air Fryer Bean Soup	-
13	Coconut Lime Soup	Roasted Tomato Soup	Kale Beef Soup	-
14	Onion Soup	Corn Soup	Healthy Bean Soup	-
15	Onion Omelet	Healthy Chicken Casserole	Grilled Sardines	Berries Mix
16	Asparagus Salad	Lemon Tuna	Shrimp & Green Beans	Apple Dumplings
17	Potato Jalapeno Hash	Sesame Seeds Coated Fish	Lemon Chicken Breast	Blueberry Lemon Muffins
18	Vegetable Quiche	Air Fried Chicken Fillets	Garlic Chicken Wings	Air Fried Apples
19	Spicy Sweet Potato Hash	Packet Lobster Tail	Herbed Baked Shrimp	Air Fried Banana with Sesame Seeds
20	Garlic Bacon Pizza	Pecan Crusted Chicken	Herb Flavored Lamb	Carrot Cake
21	Shrimp Frittata	Ground Chicken Meatballs	Chicken with Citrus Sauce	Angel Food Cake
22	Indian Cauliflower	Cajun Spiced Salmon	Creamy Chicken	Blueberry Pudding
23	Shrimp Sandwiches	Flounder Fillets	Cajun Salmon	Berry Yogurt Cake
24	Potatoes with Bacon	Shrimp, Zucchini & Cherry Tomato Sauce	Seasoned Catfish	Chocolate Mug Cake
25	Breakfast Casserole	Japanese-Style Fried Prawns	Grilled Tilapia with Portobello Mushrooms	Chocolate & Pomegranate Bars
26	Spinach Egg Breakfast	Ranch Fish Fillets	Basil Chicken	Chocolate Cake
27	Chicken & Zucchini Omelet	Garlic Herb Turkey Breast	Montreal Fried Shrimp	Chocolate Soufflé
28	Breakfast Fish Tacos	Low-Carb Fried Chicken	Monkfish with Olives & Capers	Cocoa & Almond Bars
29	Kale with Tuna	Parsley Catfish	Spiced Tilapia	Baked Apples
30	Cauliflower Mix Black Cod	Vinegar Spice Prawns	Cabbage with Salmon Fish	Apple Treat with Raisins

Conclusion

In addition to shrinking your stomach, bariatric surgery alters the path food takes through your digestive tract to reach your intestines. Following the operation, it is critical to ensure that you are getting enough nutrition while still decreasing weight. An air fryer is a convenient kitchen appliance that helps you meet the low-fat requirements of a bariatric diet. You will be able to prepare tasty & healthy surgery-safe dishes with ease & speed if you use this kitchen equipment.

Moving toward a healthy lifestyle that supports your weight-loss objectives may take time & work, but with appropriate meal planning & a flexible equipment like the air fryer, nothing is out of reach. Of course, your long-term safety & success will be determined by your frequent follow-up appointments with your surgeon & surgical team.

Index

Air Fried Apples, 84
Air Fried Banana with Sesame Seeds, 79
Air Fried Chicken Fillets, 27
Air Fried Leeks, 52
Air Fryer Bean Soup, 90
Air Fryer Chili Lime Tilapia, 42
Air-Fried Turkey Breast, 63
Angel Food Cake, 78
Appetizing Cajun Shrimp, 62
Apple Dumplings, 82
Apple Hand Pies, 81
Apple Treat with Raisins, 79
Asian Pork Soup, 89
Asparagus Salad, 22
Asparagus with Garlic, 53
Avocado Jalapeno Side Dish, 59
Baked Apples, 80
Baked Potatoes, 55
Banana Snack, 55
Basil Chicken, 63
Basil Cod, 73
Basil Tomato Soup, 89
Berries Mix, 86
Berry Yogurt Cake, 81
Blended Veggie Chips, 59
Blueberry Lemon Muffins, 87
Blueberry Pudding, 84
Breakfast Casserole, 21
Breakfast Fish Tacos, 23
Breakfast Frittata, 16
Broccoli Muffins, 19
Buttered Scallops, 733
Cabbage with Salmon Fish, 77
Cajun Chicken, 40
Cajun Salmon, 46
Cajun Spiced Salmon, 74
Carrot Cake, 86
Cauliflower Mix Black Cod, 17
Chard with Cheddar, 47
Cheese Sticks, 57
Cheesy Chicken Rolls, 55

Cheesy Chicken Wings, 61
Cheesy Roasted Sweet Potatoes, 49
Cheesy Scotch Eggs, 26
Cherry-Choco Bars, 85
Chicken & Zucchini Omelet, 23
Chicken Drumettes, 42
Chicken Drumsticks, 37
Chicken Fajitas, 65
Chicken Hash, 66
Chicken Kebabs, 70
Chicken Paprika, 69
Chicken Rice Noodle Soup, 91
Chicken Thighs, 68
Chicken Tikka Masala, 63
Chicken with Citrus Sauce, 45
Chili Squash Wedges, 53
Chocolate & Pomegranate Bars, 81
Chocolate Cake, 85
Chocolate Mug Cake, 83
Chocolate Soufflé, 79
Cocoa & Almond Bars, 82
Cocoa Banana Chips, 57
Coconut Lime Soup, 91
Cod Fish Nuggets, 77
Corn on Cobs, 48
Corn Soup, 93
Cornish Chicken, 30
Cream Potato, 54
Creamy Cabbage, 50
Creamy Chicken, 66
Creamy Potatoes, 52
Crispy Broccoli, 47
Crispy Brussels Sprouts And Potatoes, 48
Crumbly Chicken Tenderloins, 26
Delicious Mushroom Mix Side Dish, 58
Delicious Wrapped Shrimp, 61
Dill Mashed Potato, 51
Easy Tuna Patties, 44
Flounder Fillets, 28
Garlic Bacon Pizza, 20
Garlic Chicken Wings, 64

Garlic Herb Turkey Breast, 27
Garlic Lemon Shrimp, 75
Glazed Bananas, 83
Grilled Sardines, 43
Grilled Tilapia with Portobello Mushrooms, 39
Ground Chicken Meatballs, 25
Healthy Bean Soup, 88
Healthy Chicken Casserole, 34
Healthy Sausage Mix, 45
Healthy Spinach Balls, 60
Herb Flavored Lamb, 37
Herbed Baked Shrimp, 39
Herbed Trout & Asparagus, 36
Honey-Lime Chicken Wings, 66
Indian Cauliflower, 16
Japanese-Style Fried Prawns, 30
Kale Beef Soup, 92
Kale with Tuna, 18
Korean Fried Chicken, 68
Lemon & Chicken Pepper, 40
Lemon Chicken Breast, 43
Lemon Tuna, 72
Lemon-Pepper Chicken Breast, 41
Lime Air Fryer Salmon, 38
Low-Carb Fried Chicken, 64
Mind-Blowing Air-Fried Crawfish with Cajun Dipping Sauce, 33
Monkfish with Olives & Capers, 71
Montreal Fried Shrimp, 36
Mushrooms with Veggies & Avocado, 51
Onion Omelet, 18
Onion Soup, 88
Packet Lobster Tail, 31
Parsley Catfish, 29
Party Pork Rolls, 62
Pecan Crusted Chicken, 67
Pepper Egg Bites, 17
Potato Jalapeno Hash, 20
Potatoes with Bacon, 15
Ranch Fish Fillets, 32
Ricotta Cheesecake, 78
Roasted Tomato Soup, 90
Salty Lemon Artichokes, 49
Seasoned Catfish, 75
Sesame Seeds Coated Fish, 33
Shrimp & Green Beans, 76
Shrimp Frittata, 15
Shrimp Sandwiches, 20
Shrimp, Zucchini & Cherry Tomato Sauce, 72
Simple Salmon, 74
Snapper & Spring Onions, 25
Southern-Air-Fried Catfish, 76
Soy Sauce Mushrooms, 50
Spiced Tilapia, 38
Spicy Shrimp, 28
Spicy Sweet Potato Hash, 24
Spinach Egg Breakfast, 19
Spinach with Salmon & Seashells, 73
Splendid Salmon Patties, 71
Steak with Cabbage, 29
Stunning Air-Fried Clams, 31
Sweet & Sour Chicken, 32
Sweet Apple & Pear Chips, 58
Tarragon Chicken, 44
Tasty Cheese Sticks, 56
Turkey Meatballs, 69
Vegetable Quiche, 22
Vinegar Spice Prawns, 35
Zucchini Gratin, 24

Made in the USA
Las Vegas, NV
10 May 2024

89772367R00057